W0091198

FILMING HORROR

FILMING HORROR

HINDI CINEMA, GHOSTS AND IDEOLOGIES

MERAJ AHMED MUBARKI

www.sagepublishing.com

Los Angeles | London | New Delhi | Singapore | Washington DC | Melbourne

Copyright © Meraj Ahmed Mubarki, 2016

All rights reserved. No part of this book may be reproduced or utilized in any form or by any means, electronic or mechanical, including photocopying, recording or by any information storage or retrieval system, without permission in writing from the publisher.

Screenshots used by the author in the book are for representational purposes only.

First published in 2016 by

 SAGE Publications India Pvt Ltd
B1/I-1 Mohan Cooperative Industrial Area
Mathura Road, New Delhi 110 044, India
www.sagepub.in

SAGE Publications Inc
2455 Teller Road
Thousand Oaks, California 91320, USA

SAGE Publications Ltd
1 Oliver's Yard, 55 City Road
London EC1Y 1SP, United Kingdom

SAGE Publications Asia-Pacific Pte Ltd
3 Church Street
#10-04 Samsung Hub
Singapore 049483

Published by Vivek Mehra for SAGE Publications India Pvt Ltd, typeset in 11/13 pts Book Antiqua by RECTO Graphics, Delhi and printed at Chaman Enterprises, New Delhi.

Library of Congress Cataloging-in-Publication Data

Names: Mubarki, Meraj Ahmed author.
Title: Filming horror: Hindi cinema, ghosts and ideologies/Meraj Ahmed Mubarki.
Description: New Delhi ; Thousand Oaks : SAGE Publications, 2016. | Includes
   bibliographical references and index.
Identifiers: LCCN 2015049016| ISBN 9789351508724 (hardback : alk. paper) |
   ISBN 9789351508717 (epub : alk. paper) | ISBN 9789351508731 (ebook : alk.
   paper)
Subjects: LCSH: Motion pictures—India—History. | Horror films—India—
   History and criticism. | Motion pictures—Social aspects—India.
Classification: LCC PN1993.5.I8 M65 2016 | DDC 791.430954—dc23 LC record
available at http://lccn.loc.gov/2015049016

ISBN: 978-93-515-0872-4 (HB)

The SAGE Team: Shambhu Sahu, Isha Sachdeva and Vinitha Nair

*Dedicated to my mother Umida Begum and
to the memory of my father, the late Md Ahmed Mubarki,
film distributor and a fanatic horror film buff*

Thank you for choosing a SAGE product!
If you have any comment, observation or feedback,
I would like to personally hear from you.
Please write to me at **contactceo@sagepub.in**

Vivek Mehra, Managing Director and CEO, SAGE India.

Bulk Sales

SAGE India offers special discounts
for purchase of books in bulk.
We also make available special imprints
and excerpts from our books on demand.

For orders and enquiries, write to us at

Marketing Department
SAGE Publications India Pvt Ltd
B1/I-1, Mohan Cooperative Industrial Area
Mathura Road, Post Bag 7
New Delhi 110044, India

E-mail us at **marketing@sagepub.in**

Get to know more about SAGE

Be invited to SAGE events, get on our mailing list.
Write today to **marketing@sagepub.in**

This book is also available as an e-book.

Contents

List of Figures

Preface

The 'seed' of this book germinated in Kolkata, and parts of the initial work were written out during my association with Shri Shikshayatan College. The idea of a book on Hindi horror cinema was tested in a series of articles, and the responses to those publications assured me that a full-scale documentation of the Hindi horror genre was feasibly overdue. This encouraged me to undertake a wider approach encompassing the genre in all its forms and expressions. In this regard, I wish to acknowledge that arguments made in the book have appeared in 'Mapping the Hindi Horror Genre: Ghosts in the Service of Ideology' in *History and Sociology of South Asia* (Vol. 7, Issue: 1, January 2013); 'The Monstrous "Other" Feminine: Gender, Desire and the "Look" in the Hindi Horror Genre' in the *Indian Journal of Gender Studies* (Vol. 21, Issue: 3, October 2014); and 'Monstrosities of Science: Exploring Monster Narratives in Hindi Horror Cinema' in *Visual Anthropology* (Vol. 28, Issue: 3, 2015).

Acknowledgements

I would like to thank associates, colleagues, the Saiyid Hamid Library staff and the administration at Maulana Azad National Urdu University, Hyderabad, for creating an environment that made this endeavour possible. I would like to thank students, friends and colleagues at Shri Shikshayatan College, the British Council Library and the American Information Resource Center (AIRC) in Kolkata. I would like to thank the following for their words of encouragement and help in ways that need to be acknowledged here: Shambhu Sahu of SAGE Publications (for his support, enthusiasm and for awarding me with newer deadlines every time I failed to meet old ones); Jyotsna Kapur, Southern Illinois University (whose suggestions on a part of this project in its incipient form helped me sharpen my arguments); Paul Hockings, University of Illinois, Chicago (for help and assistance that goes beyond this book); Tabassum 'Ruhi' Khan, University of California, Riverside; Ira Bhasker and Bishupriya Dutt, Jawaharlal Nehru University; Tapati Basu and S. N. Bera, University of Calcutta; Steve Menezes (Steve Sir), St. Anthony's High School; Jaysri Ray (Jaysri Di), Anuradha Banerjee (Anuradha Di), Debjani Nag (Debjani Di) at Shri Shikshayatan College; the anonymous reviewers at *History and Sociology of South Asia, Indian Journal of Gender Studies and Visual Anthropology* and at SAGE Publications. Thanks are due to my students Ritwika Mitra and Sreemoyee Bagchi for their initial readings and very cheering words of encouragement. Thanks go out to Rajuan, Nazma Bhabhi, Bobbian, Zeenat, Gullo (Naah), Shirin Baji, Nazeer Bhai, Arshad Bhai, Bushra, Zayaan (who is addicted to horror fiction), Ayaan, Armaan, Dania, Fuzail, my father-in-law Hafiz Ali, Saquib, Rizwana, Rushdi, Ruhi, Mudassar, Hammad and Hafsa. Thanks go out to Rakhi Lahiri (Rakhi Di), Sagnik Basu, Somali Chowdhury, Subir Chakraborty, Manasi Sengupta and to Obaid Hassan Dugman, who would initially ridicule my ideas, and then back them anyway because of our long and enduring friendship.

Finally, this book would not have been possible without the active support of Subuhi who endured long periods of my absence, but without whom this endeavour would have never seen the light of day. I hope Aymaan will, someday, read this book.

1

Indian Cinema and Ideology

Hindi cinema has been much subjected to academic insights in the preceding two decades by Chidananda Dasgupta (1991), Sumita Chakravarty (1993), Ashish Rajadhyaksha (1999) and M. Madhava Prasad (2000), among others. Genre studies of Hindi cinema have emerged as an important area of academic interest. But Hindi horror cinema with its own aesthetics, rituals and structural conventions has escaped academic attention and needs to be studied in its own right. The book tries to incorporate and explore the various strands of the Hindi horror genre and reconnoitre the broad conditions of its (sub)generic possibilities in terms of the discourses they espouse. The book seeks to understand the emergence and contemporary articulations of the genre made possible by larger social forces at work within the discursive practices of imagining the Indian nation, marking moments of continuity and disruption within the genre.

This effort aims to draw attention to the Hindi horror genre, discover its narrative strategies, frame methodology of analyses, probe the transformations taking place within the genre and contemplate on the means that the genre uses to counter the monster/ghost. The book tries to bridge the gap that currently exists in the field. And though there may inevitably be disagreements with the construals offered here, it should serve to open the debate rather than restrict it.

Hindi Cinema and Ideology

Susan Hayward posits: 'Cinema is an ideological apparatus by nature of its very seamlessness. We do not see how it produces meaning—it renders it invisible, naturalizes it. Mainstream or dominant cinema, in Hollywood and elsewhere puts ideology up onscreen' (Hayward, 1996, p. 182). Others have hinted at the inherently ideological nature of cinema discernible in its mode of production and consumption. Through realistic images and sound and the perspectival space projected on screen, cinema creates double illusion: first, the finished product disguises how its production technology has fashioned cinema; second, at the level of consumption, cinema fashions the subject—spectatorship that identifies itself with the camera, the apparatus that has looked at before, what the spectator is looking at presently. The filmic text further sutures the spectatorship in the narrative through cinematic conventions such as the subjective camera angle that enmeshes the viewer into the plot, the shot–reverse shot that seals the subject through view and counter viewpoint, and specifically the continuity of editing that imparts seamlessness into the narrative and tides over disconnection between time and space by imparting cinematic uniformity and flatness.

Even if cinema was introduced in India by the Lumiere Brothers' short films on 7 July 1896 at Bombay's Watson Hotel, Indians were quick to adapt to cinema. The Indian Cinematograph Committee of 1927–28 noted that 'Indians gain the cinema sense very quickly — the uneducated sometimes more quickly than the educated' (Mazzarella, 2009, p. 66). The cultural roots for this appreciation of cinema can be traced back to the highly stylized Sanskrit plays fixated upon the idea of an elaborate and remarkable display of spectacle: 'Ostentatious display that temporarily arrest the flow of narrative' (Brown, 2011, p. 51). With their moralistic overtones, principles of wisdom to the accompaniment of ritualized song-and-dance routine, the popular Indian cinema is the natural inheritance of Sanskrit theatre. The Sanskrit plays themselves drew heavily from the two great Hindu epics of the *Ramayana* and the *Mahabharata*. Invariably, supernatural and magical elements became integral to the plots as many principal characters were either accursed or bewitched or both.

Since Sanskrit theatre received state patronage, their fate was tied up with the vicissitudes of the ruling political class and caste, and thus the loss of political authority by the patrons around the 12th century AD meant the decline of Sanskrit plays. However, other regional variants such as the *Bhavai* in Gujarat, *Jatra* in Bengal, *Yakshagana* in Karnataka, *Vithinatakam* of Andhra Pradesh, and the *Ram Lila* and *Krishna Lila* of Uttar Pradesh emerged soon after. Though crude and sometimes unsophisticated, these performing arts preserved and embodied some principles and elements of the original Sanskrit plays, often reworking the essence of the Sanskrit theatre in new theatrical dialects. But Sanskrit theatre was quasi-religious and ritualistic in its mode of presentation, often employing the elements of dance and gesture to describe the physical settings or the locale of divine action. The regional performing arts were mostly performed in open avenues. Live performances such as *Terukkuttu* of Tamil Nadu conflate the religious with the social whereby the staging of the act is 'at once entertainment, an act of worship, a medium of social instructions, transmitter of epical myths and socio-religious festival, where the actors are believed to become the abode of divinity during the period of performance' (Varadpande, 1992, p. 39). Visual representations remained central to the subcontinent's cultural practices.

Sandria B. Freitag traces this origin of visual images as 'the shapers and bearers of thought' (Freitag, 2001, p. 39) to the realm of courtly culture, religious practices that implied *darshan* and live enactments of a public nature such as *ramlilas, nautanki,* etc. Further, the concept of *badnazar* or evil eye often interpreted as mere coup d'oeil that can cause serious afflictions and bodily harms marks the ocular centricity of South Asian culture practices. Even *darshan* is not restricted to Hindus alone. While the centrality of the Hindu act of worship implies mutual exchange between the *bhakt* and the deity, the introduction of lithography liberalized and democratized visual culture to include belief systems such as Islam that abhors representation, as the ubiquitous presence of pictures of the Holy Kabah in Muslim households in the subcontinent would testify. Moreover, the Indian subcontinent provides many opportunities for an ostentatious display of religious iconography ranging from the displayed photographs of tombs of Muslim saints at Muslim homes to that of the frescoes of *Buraaq*,[1] the mythical horse that took the Holy Prophet on his ascension to heaven, supposedly bestowing divine benevolence on the 'spectator-believer'.

But it was the Parsi theatre whose emergence in the 1850s brought diverse European techniques and the Indian storytelling proficiencies together in highly spectacle-oriented plays; it was performed in proscenium theatres, where the audience could directly face the stage, which itself had been raised several feet above the audience level. These proscenium theatres allowed for a variety of props and backdrops to be used in consonance with the play being enacted, thus sanctioning for a more realistic interpretation of the stories. Parsi theatre became an important conduit in connecting large urban audiences. The middle-class audience for these Parsi theatres was aided and abetted by colonial Bombay's assorted English and Gujarati newspapers which displayed advertisements, commented avidly on their performances, and created a furore around the fledgling theatre (Hansen, 2002). Parsi theatre introduced new spectatorial experiences for the audience. Backgrounds and costumes could be changed with the dropping of the curtains, allowing for the emergence of a chronological narrative experience. The Parsi theatre could unhinge explicit Hindu mythology from drama as it went beyond the traditional narratives from the mythological Hindu epics and introduced rich transnational grand narratives such as the *Arabian Nights*, Ferdowsi's *Shahnama*, Urdu and Gujarati renditions of Shakespearian tragedies, and Victorian melodramas to reach out to a much wider audience. This does not suggest their apolitical affiliation since travelling theatres were popular nationalist devices and many troupes 'financially contributed to revolutionary outfits in the late nineteenth and twentieth centuries' (Benei, 2008, p. 103. ff 9).

As the theatres diversified, they picked up social themes and laid the foundation for various genres. The performative grammar of the cinema that emerged later in the early twentieth century with the pioneering effort of Dadasaheb Phalke was no different from the theatre that had emerged in the preceding decades. Parsi theatre acted as a conduit between the 'pre-modern theatrical' and the later 'cinematic melodramatic' that followed, priming audience expectation and homogenizing spectatorial conventions through its modes of presentation. Cinema aided the *pre-cinematic* visual culture of *darshanic* gaze involving anthropomorphic cartography,[2] which often depicted the embryonic nation-state in terms of a divine feminine imparting familiarity and recognizability to the nation-state. Lithographic printing circulated veiled and seditious images whose 'relevance to a colonized India would have been lost on few' (Pinney, 2009, p. 34). The ubiquitous print media created a nationalized consciousness priming the pliant and colonized citizenry for a nationalist discourse. And although the process of defining national cinema is a 'work in progress', cinema only produces an ever-incomplete nation; it can 'apparently reflect and keep in circulation values and behaviour associated with a particular nation' (Williams, 2002, p. 8).

Cinema in the Colonial Context

The cinema that emerged in the colonial context was largely imported, and emerging Indian filmmakers who had to compete with imported cinema invariably saw themselves as being engaged in a nationalist enterprise. European producers exercised economies of scale and competitive advantage over their Indian counterparts aided in no small measure by the easy flow of advanced global capital across borders, greater accessibility to overseas audiences, and larger markets at their disposal that went beyond the subcontinent. They could, therefore, offer their films for exhibition in Indian theatres at inferior exhibition rates. Mythological films based on Indian folklores likewise offered contextual advantage to Indian filmmakers, and 'Indian silent cinema was constructed on a Hindu religious address' (Hughes, 2006, p. 51), which despite the anticolonial movement's efforts 'to preserve intercommunity amity Indian cinema was permeated by a Hindu narrative right from its inception' (Benei, 2008, p. 85).

India's first film, *Raja Harishchandra* (King Harishchandra) (Phalke, 1913) drew on an overtly Hindu religious theme and was produced and directed by Dadasaheb Phalke who 'was influenced by an early film on the life of Jesus Christ and had a strong belief that Hindu mythology must be retold in ways relevant to the age' (Wright, 2007, p. 149). His explicit purpose 'was to create an Indian national cinema by adapting Hindu mythological stories for the screen' (Hughes, 2006, p. 51). In his own words, Phalke was 'gripped by a strange spell ... could we the sons of India ever be able to see Indian images on the screen? (Rajadhyaksha, 1999, p. 131). Phalke's founding film was followed by well-known episodes from the Hindu Puranas, such as *Mohini Bhasmasur* (1913), *Satyavan Savitri* (1914), *Lanka Dahan* (1917), *Shri Krishna Janma* (1918) and *Kaliya Mardan* (1919). Nativist cinema thus reenacted scenes which the colonial system's secular modernity wanted Indians to abandon. Far from inducing contemporaneity 'the mytho-logical genre gave access for the Hindu pantheon to this powerful instrument of belief; [and] instead of retreating before science as in the West, Indian Gods obtained new life from it' (Dasgupta, 1989, p. 14). It could transcend the restriction of language and be comprehensible to the diverse linguistic groups of the subcontinent. Not only did cinema render Hindu mythology in mass circulation accessible in newer forms through the nature of cinematic imagination, it augmented the extant auditory and visual resources by re-enacting the Hindu legends, imparting a celluloid-mediated reincarnation to common visual representation of divini-ties, bestowing homogeneity to a diversity of mythological constructions in circulation.

The most potent visual manifestation of the colonial con-text was the 'empire cinema', or the British and American films oscillating between oriental exoticism and imperial concerns made specifically during the 1930s and 1940s that 'presented ideological concerns and images in keeping with this imperial vision' (Chowdhry, 2000, p. 1). The Empire film trope drawing upon a tradition of pro-imperial literature consolidated the idea of the British Empire as a benign con-sensual hegemony and naturalized the colonial gaze as just, benign and necessary in the colonial context. If the British production *The Drum* directed by Zoltan Korda depicted British rule 'as a way of protecting the Indian masses from the threat of Muslim extremism' (Sinha B., 2011, p. 542), *Gunga Din* trivialized the recumbent colonial Indian nation-alism as Hindu nationalism in which 'the professedly saintly and pacifist of the Hindu villain had a hidden agenda to violently overthrow the British rule and impose Hindu rule (Chowdhry, 2000, p. 132). Phalke's offering of well-known mythological stories to Indian audiences invoking common cultural legacies could later be politicized by the emergent nationalist freedom movement.

Paralleling other public spaces such as the railway stations, bus *addas*, *bazaars* and the ubiquitous *dak ghar*, cinema opened up the opportunities of equal access to its patron that transcended prior feudal spatial practices, at a time when temples, residential expanses and even water sources had restricted public access. Its egalitarian effect must, however, be qualified with the fact that cinema imposed new forms of segregations based on ticket pricing and gender. Thus, even within the imperial narrative of power, the cinemas appeared as a decolonizing agency. Cinema also imparted a sense of recognizability to the anonymous multitudes thronging Indian theatres, imposing on them the qualities of an emerging ethnographic state that coalesced at show times only to disperse after it. If cinema came to acquire the aura of faith, theatres acquired a quasi-religious halo of congregations where the faithful could assemble for collective social experiences. For the urban majority, cinematic gods in the mythological became a subtle spiritual aid and gave Indian cinema 'a quasi-religious tenor utterly without parallel in the West' (Dasgupta, 1989, p. 13).

But perhaps even more troubling was the 'reversal of gaze' that cinema afforded to Indian audiences during colonial times. The large number of American films exhibited in India in the 1920s had to be censored to be rendered suitable for the native's consumption. Imported cinema especially American films with their visuals of moral excesses raised cultural concerns on either side of the imperial divide. If the European community feared that the American cinema and its moral excesses might be construed as a way of life in the West and bring the Western civilization into disrepute, Indian cultural hygienists wanted strict control on cinematic expressions fearing that imported cinema threatened the extant, traditional and moral economy of the masses through visuals of moral depravity and corruption. While the colonial authority recognized the potential of cinema and its ability to reach out to a much wider viewership with far greater effect where, 'every device is employed in order to intensify the visual impression, such as the well-known device of the close up' (Indian Cinematograph Committee, 1928, p. 1), it also knew the inherent risk that cinema could trivialize the imperial order and misrepresent the Western civilization.

As the Indian Cinematograph Committee noted,

> American civilization is as much Western civilization to them [Indian audiences] as British civilization. Both are foreign. If there is a misunderstanding ... of American scenes shown in the films and confusion of them with European civilization, more especially British civilization it is because they [Indian audiences] regard them all as one. (Indian Cinematograph Committee, 1928, p. 99)

Nevertheless, to reduce Hollywood cinema's cultural and economic dominance, the Cinematograph Films Act of 1927 imposed quota on the number of films that could be imported into the British Empire.

By the 1930s, cinema became another aesthetic link between popular culture and the rallying freedom struggle. With its subjectivity and close-ups, cinema symbolically allowed for a subversive appropriation of images of whiteness by providing access to hitherto inaccessible recesses of the Empire, namely the private lives of the imperium accentuating imperial anxieties and surreptitiously bringing down the edifice of remoteness and inapproachability that the imperial order had assiduously created and maintained since the eruption of open hostilities with Indians in 1857. Cinema also allowed for the crossing over of the spatial–temporal divide between the imperial and the national. While seeking to limit the excesses of a censoring authority, the remedy as the Home Secretary H. G. Haig pointed out lay, 'in a considerable extension of the production of Indian films—showing Indian stories in an Indian setting' (Indian

Cinematograph Committee, 1928, p. 8). It was hoped that with the production of better Indian films, 'the exclusive preference for Western films shown by a certain section of the audience, both European and Indian, will … gradually disappear (Indian Cinematograph Committee, 1928, p. 70). Encouragement of Indian films therefore especially 'the "mythological" [was] seen as a way of keeping the low class of Indians away from the theatres that show[ed] western films' (Prasad, 2004, p. 165). Reinforcement of indigenous Indian films by the British Imperial System was, therefore, not shorn of colonial logic. It was hoped that British Indian cinema would move in guided direction, maintaining the spatiotemporal distance between the Empire and its subjects.

The narrative trajectories of pre-Independence cinema created its subject viewer in diverse ways: attracting and coalescing some and repelling and frittering away others. The Indian Cinematograph Committee noted that whereas educated Indians aligned with imperial interests idealized the imported American and British films as a mark of their distance from the masses, the ordinary masses preferred Indian films retelling ancient Hindu mythological tales howsoever 'tackily' produced. The prosaic response of the 'classy' audiences from the balconies would be equally matched by the kinetic boisterousness of the galleries; the urban poor came to represent the strongest constituency of indigenous Hindi mythological cinema.

Spectatorship became a site not just of class differences and social hierarchies but also communal identities. Mythological cinema was apparently less affected by provincial differences than films of other genres and was uniquely positioned to appeal to the majority of Hindu Indians, who despite their cultural and linguistic departures shared common mythological experiences. For many Indians, the mythologicals were 'a celebration of India's spiritual superiority and an affirmation of a distinctive national culture' (Hughes, 2006, p. 54). Because of the authority that cinema imparts to the moving image, mythological films with their modest mechanism of identification, chequered narrative continuities, and closures allowed for a homogenization of the Hindu myths operating extra-diegetically without the screen. Whereas the introduction of sound technology provided a sort of natural protection against foreign film domination over Indian markets the 'talkies' demanded primary linguistic identification from its public. The introduction of sound fragmented the audience along linguistic lines and put pressure on producers to innovate through diversified genres. With the concurrent decline in enthusiasm for the mythologicals, studios scaled back their investments in the *puranic* tales and expanded their repertoire to include other genres: the historical, the social, the stunt and the folklore, that came of age in the subsequent decades. It is no coincidence the emergence of genres coincided with the introduction of sound in Indian cinema.

Mythological cinema created restricted viewership since Hindu mythologicals had limited appeal for Muslim spectatorship, as the manager of a theatre in Madras noted wryly about the cold reception meted out to Hindu mythologicals in a Madras locality: 'Most of our patrons on that side are Mohammedans and they do not care much for Indian films' (Indian Cinematograph Committee, Vol. 3, p. 376 quoted in Hughes, 2006, p. 60).

Whereas the precolonial historical cinema with its anti-colonial ideological stance did attempt to bolster 'the mainstream nationalist rhetoric of syncretic, pluralistic and secular tradition of the country' (Bhaskar & Allen, 2009, p. 25), it is also appropriate to note that concomitant with instances of cinematic attempts to 'represent' the medieval period as an era of sycreticism, especially with reference to historical films, mostly featuring Mughal Emperors, was the need to assert the primacy of the community over the national space which led to the sphere of public performativity becoming an area of aggressive contests. These cinematic attempts were viewed by the Right as attempts to 'whitewash Muslim intolerance in Mughal days' and 'plea for Pakistan' (Mukhopadhyay, 2008, p. 66). Concurrent with the opening up of Hindi-speaking market for cinema were Hindi films featuring the Rajput legends. But with luke-warm box office appeal for internal Rajput palace intrigues, producers of this genre eventually 'reverted to the [themes of] heroic resistance posed by the 'Hindu' Rajputs against Muslim invaders' (Mukhopadhyay, 2008, p. 69).

The Muslim League questioned the intention of non-Muslim directors in presenting Muslim themes, and in 1933 a Muslim League legislator raised a question in the Assembly regarding 'the censorship of cinematograph films calculated to offend Muslim sentiments' (Dwyer, 2006, p. 114). Cinema came under increased scrutiny and 'the religious identity of producers, directors and actors was being related to the on-screen narratives and in fact was seen to continue a critical social and political level to the narrative' (Vasudevan, 2000, p. 156).

In 1937, an All India League for Censorship was formed with the aim to 'cleanse the film industry of all its non-Hindu elements' and 'extended to the question of who should control the means of representation' (Mishra, 2002, p. 217). Historical films depicting the ongoing nationalist struggle in allegorical but communal terms failed to create 'fictive unity' and often ran into trouble with sections of the audience with different historical experiences and grievances for whom the courageous exploits of one liege lord was the ruthless ravages of the other. Although such conflicting interpretations of history had existed before the introduction of cinema in India, specifically in the local folk chronicles and often circulated within their respective specific spheres of ethnicities being passed on from generation to generation, films created the spatial convergence where these folk histories could be visualized, projected and brought into conflict with each other. Through the apparatus of the camera, cinema endowed the Hindu mythology with a homogenous texture and allowed for the emergence of a standardized mythological narrative, imparting Semitic properties to largely heterogeneously organized Hindu scriptural narratives.

By imparting the mythologies with a never before sense of reality, cinema imposed the national over the provincial, and the visual over the aural, literally prefiguring the popularity of the mythologicals in the 1970s, particularly *Jai Santoshi Maa* (Hail Mother Goddess Santoshi) (Sharma, 1975) which 'established the Goddess Santoshi as a popular deity among working-class women in urban centres, which [were] rapidly increasing and where knowledge of traditional rituals [was] decreasing' (Wright, 2007, p. 149). Thus, Hindi cinema has always been a project of cultural nationalism and from its inception was placed in an oppositional mode to the cinema from overseas. The pioneering cinematic efforts by early Indian filmmakers such as V. Shantaram, K. Subrahmanyam, M. Bhavnani, Sohrab Modi and J. B. H. Wadia during the Raj (Pre-Independence) era necessarily became a cultural force multiplier in the all-pervading project of the nation-state. Early filmmakers were not just producing films, they were engaged in *swadeshi* or indigenous enterprise as an alternative to imported cinema, turning the screen into an imaginary nation space. Indian filmmakers saw their on-screen projections as part of a grand patriotic scheme. In these ways, Indian cinema was imbricated within the project of articulating a nationalist agenda however defined.

Notes

1. The *Buraaq* is popularly represented as a fabulous monster endowed with wings, a woman's head and the body of a horse.
2. This has been further explored by Sumathi Ramaswamy; see (Ramaswamy, 2001)

2

Genre, Codes and the Horror Cinema

Before embarking on an enquiry about horror cinema and its generic mutations, it is pertinent to understand a range of views on cinematic imaginations and its relation to larger discourses within a given system and parcel out the contributions of evolving sociopolitical determinants, the studio systems, the predilections of the *auteur* and the audience's preferences. What and to which extent does each of the determinants decide upon the film's content? If the critical theory espoused by the Frankfurt School emphasized the role of sociopolitical determinants in limiting the use of imagination, either cinematic or otherwise, it envisioned passive audiences submitting uncritically to an all-dominating apparatus mesmerized by the illusionist power of cinema. The school held that generic cinema allowed for efficiency of mass production and familiarity of ease of consumption, creating passivity and conformity in the audience leaving no room for interpretive freedom. But in the 1950s, a series of articles in the French journal *Cahier Du cinema* championed film directors as *auteurs* whose, 'personality or personal creative vision could be read thematically and stylistically across their body of work (Kuhn & Westwell, 2012, p. 26). The *auteur* theory positioned the director 'as a specific, subjective psychological cause whose free will, desires, beliefs, and intentions consciously structure a film' (Buckland, 2012, p. 22). Through their individual styles the auteurs could define, subvert and ironize the formulaic materials.

Structuralism sought to replace the *auteur's* free will with 'general causes that determine the meaning of individual utterances, artworks, or films' (Buckland, 2012, p. 22). Structuralism argued that like myths and folktales, genres had deep cultural roots and provided audiences with structured ways of understanding social experiences, through oft-repeated stories. And genre's functionality in contemporary society paralleled myths and legends in pre-modern societies, reiterating, renewing and retelling the genre's core myths in distinctive ways, which could be used to understand dominant ideologies and wider sociocultural and historical changes. Genres like myths presented 'the way in which a particular culture ha[d] embodied both mythical archetypes and its own preoccupations in narrative forms' (Real, 1989). If mythology was organized into binary oppositions of two mutually exclusive terms, genres like mythical thoughts always progressed 'from the awareness of oppositions towards their resolutions' (Levi-Strauss, 1963, p. 224).

So, where did it leave the directors and their visionary statement whose centrality to film production was advanced by the *auteur* theory? The *auteur* simply actualized one possible combination from a series of a codes and conventions of a given underlying system. In the words of Levi-Strauss, 'the apparent arbitrariness of the mind, its supposedly spontaneous flow of inspiration, and its seemingly uncontrolled inventiveness imply the existence of laws operating at a deeper level' (Levi-Strauss, 1970, p. 10). By the 1960s and the 1970s genre criticism abjured the role of the *auteur* and sought to examine the recurrent themes, motifs and iconographies circumscribing the authorial intentionality that had marked cinema studies of the 1950s. Further undermining the *auteur*istic vision was the psychoanalyst deconstructionist theory which argued that even subjectivity was not intrinsic, essentialist, or ahistorical but was instead produced by our entry into social formations and symbolic systems that preexisted our consciousness. 'Consciousness and "reality" were thus socially, culturally, and historically specific' (Sconce, 1993, p. 108). And 'when what one is looking for is a set of objective structures, the role of the author as subjectivity becomes almost peripheral' (Nowell-Smith, 1970, p. 133).

Directors/production houses/studios did not consciously produce dominant discourse but rather as historical subjects unconsciously 'reiterated' it and adopted axiomatic ideological positions. Ideology was 'a function of the discourse and of the logic of social processes, rather than an intention of the agent' (Hall, 1982, p. 88) reducing the ideological slant to a largely unconscious phenomenon constructed by the agent 'in the absence of any intention to distort and oppress' (Hall, 1982). Foucault further posits that 'power even if exercised without aims and objectives, is the consequence of a discourse and doesn't mean that it results from the choice or decision of an individual subject' (1978, pp. 94–95). Understood in this way genres served the ritualistic purpose of providing fantastic solutions to a society's constitutive internal contradictions, produced at the behest of a specific audience. But this approach left out the most important constituency of cinema studies: the audience, which played an active role in the construction of meaning.

In the 1970s, Tom Ryall (1978) introduced a triangulation of *auteur*, social reality and the audience pointing out that the generic conventions operated through a frame of 'patterns/forms/styles/structures, which act as a form of "supervision" over the work of production of film-makers and the work of reading by an audience' (Gledhill, 1999, p. 137). This approach allowed for an assortment of determinants to be acknowledged for imparting meaning to the cinema, 'without foreclosing on the question of which element dominates in any given instance' (Gledhill, 1999, p. 138). This approach therefore allowed all the productive elements to partake in the process; the director became as important as the discourse. Later, semiotics and the concept of 'radical reading' problematized the consensus that the ideological construction of a genre be tied to its socio-historical reality; for if there be multiple construction of meanings—between a 'then' original period of a film's release and a 'now' more contemporary moment—then should the film be tied to how it was perceived by its audiences then or to a more contemporary perception? The answer lies in acknowledging the potentiality of multiple significations of the performativity of films reading and concurrently honouring the cultural context of the historical conditions of production and consumption. More recently individual genres are being looked upon not as a group of artefacts but as a discourse: 'a loose evolving system of arguments and readings, helping to shape commercial strategies and aesthetic ideologies' (Naremore, 1995, p. 14).

Genre and Its Functionality

If cinema is a 'fleeting' social moment, and the audience, an abstract group constantly constituted and reconstituted with each film going experience, genre is used to help cultivate and define the always-indeterminate anthropology of film spectatorship. Genres involve 'systems of orientations, expectations and conventions that circulate between industry, text and subject' (Neale, 1980, p. 19). The most immediate way in which viewers identify films is through their narrative structures, which refers to 'strategies, codes, and conventions employed to organize a story' (Hayward, 1996, p. 282). Genre criticism or the study of genre in cinema studies sought to classify films according to their textual form of style, iconography content, the industrial practices of production and marketing, and reception of audiences' expectations and responses (Kuhn & Westwell, 2012). Classification allowed audiences 'access' to cinema and aesthetic devices acted as cues letting the viewers know what to expect. The predictability of these devices, repetitions of plots, storyline, builds up in films and a set of particular films come to acquire conventions that separate them from other similarity-organized films. Originality is to be welcomed but only 'in the degree that it intensifies the expected experience without fundamentally altering it' (Warshow, 2002, p. 100). Genres emerge thus, implying a general limited control that directors exercised over movies, hedged in the larger but discrete social, political and economic forces at work. Yet, despite their predictability, generic films must maintain 'individualistic' difference in terms of audience expectancy. Genres must confirm and evolve upon audience anticipations, reinforcing and challenging codes and conventions simultaneously, since they must develop continuously genres must discard old conventions and adopt new ones.

However, if genres are inwardly oriented variously seeking to order a range of films through the taxonomy of a relatively stable set of narratives rules and aesthetic principles, Bakhtin argues, 'an essential (constitutive) marker of the utterance is its quality of being directed to someone, its *addressivity*.... Each speech genre ... has its own typical conception of the addressee, and this defines it as a genre (Bakhtin, 1986, p. 95)'. Each film exhibition becomes a performative act addressing a precise audience within a definite time and place under specific sociohistorical conditions. Genres are thus fashioned as much by the spectating subject who is implicated in the larger socioeconomic realities as the studios wherefrom films are produced.

For generic films, matching audience's taste with patronizing audiences is a matter of survival and if films belonging to the same genre do not innovate they tend to become formulaic and stale. Therefore, innovation in terms of plot summarization, camera techniques, is needed to impart variations. This led to a rediscovery of the film director and reconciliation between genre and *auteur* possibilities. The auteur 'individualize[d] the text, characterize[d] it and even g[ave] it its value' (Caughie, 1981, p. 127). By imparting variations, the director, as 'an element innocuous in itself, [had the] potential to initiate a complex reaction when dropped into the mix of other elements' (Andrew, 1993, p. 77). 'Auteur signature' or individual style of film directors played an important role in imparting variation and innovation.

How do genres mutate and transform nationally and internationally? The vicissitudes of sociopolitical changes, changing consumer preferences, and dynamic political forces at large often influence upon genres producing alterations, mutations, transfigurations of plots, storylines, aesthetics, etc. Consider a spate of cinepatriotic and nationalistic films in the 1960s, bearing generic similarities and thematic preoccupations that came in at a specific time in Indian history when the Indian State faced credible threats to its viability and was grappling with external threats from China and Pakistan. As a cultural commodity which relates to its own social context given that the consumer and the producer share common ideological field of experience, any genre analysis is incomplete without taking into account the conditions of consumption of films and its relationship to ideology.

The capital intensive film industry's compulsion aimed at maximization of profits does not call for too much experimentation and production houses have to ensure decent returns on investments, further reinforcing generic conventions. Overtime, films within one genre become *mimetic* responses. Bigger investment means greater risks; producers thus tend to minimize risks by offering what has been appreciated in the past, repeating narrative models, genres and plot strategies, which sometimes degenerate into remakes or generational clichés. Genres also develop out of the problem of uncertainty. Since production houses/ directors are not sure about the preferences of the audiences, they usually resort to a previous hit formula. The more one is familiar with the codes and conventions the easier it is to participate on the screen. When a genre-defying film is accepted by audiences, it attains the status of a cult classic. A successful film will trigger 'a process of attempted genre constitution in which the production house will test a series of hypotheses regarding the specific source of success leading to a full-fledged industry wide genre' (Altman, 1997, p. 283).

Horror Genre and Spectatorship

If the horror films work on distinct but not-too-hard-to-guess generic clichés, and the audiences know about the broad permutations why do they like horror films? Without homogenizing the possibilities of a range of scopophilic pleasures and subject positions that a heterogeneous spectatorship may derive from the horror genre, viewers' response of fear and the knowledge of its artificiality are not mutually exclusive. S/he knows that what frightens him/her is not real. Andrew Tudor defines broadly two distinct kinds of appeals of horror. While one set of appeal is grounded in the gratification of some preestablished fundamental human bestial needs for bloodletting that needs moments of catharsis, another set of appeal of horror lies in its ability to reflect distinct moments of social history through specific aesthetic and textual features (Tudor, 1997). For some theorists, the morbid appeal of horror can been traced to the innate seamier, darker, repressed side of the human psyche; 'to fear anxiety, sadism and masochism (Brophy, 1986, p. 5); to the genre's 'ability to dramatize all that is repressed within a society (Wood, 2003); to 'its function as a rites of passage for its mostly adolescent audience making a hormone-soaked transition from onanism to reproductive sexuality' (Twitchell, 1985, p. 65); to 'the audience's desire to throw out, eject the abject from the safety of the spectator's seat' (Creed, 2002, p. 10). Stephen King hints that horror acts as a catharsis allowing us to feel normal and remote from gore and mayhem that forms so much a part of human psyche.

> Anti-civilization emotions don't go away, and they demand periodic exercise. ... The mythic horror movie, like the sick joke, has a dirty job to do. It deliberately appeals to all that is worst in us. It is morbidity unchained, our most base instincts let free, our nastiest fantasies realized ... and it all happens, fittingly enough, in the dark. (King, n.d.)

Variously, others like Jonathan Lake Crane find the Freudian interpretive possibilities as limited and claim there is more to horror 'than thwarted libidinal desire or some other variation of psychic upheaval' (Crane, 1994, p. vi). Noel Carroll claims that the 'impossibility' of the ghost/monster elicits curiosity. But since cinematic curiosity can be aroused by other narrative forms such as murder mysteries or suspense thrillers as well, he draws a distinction:

> Horror fiction is a special variation on this general narrative motivation, because it has at the center of it something which is given as in principle unknowable—something which, *ex-hypothesi,* cannot given the structure of our conceptual scheme, exist and that cannot have the properties it has. (Carroll, 1990, p. 182)

The monster frightens us with its 'categorically interstitial, categorically contradictory, incomplete[ness] or formless[ness]' (Carroll, 1990, p. 35), and the horror film primarily seeks engagement with the audience both effectively and viscerally as it aims 'to scare and disgust, to raise the hair on the back of our necks or make us cover our eyes' (Sobchack, 1996, p. 316). The pleasure of the horror text derives from both novelty and familiarity—the audience knows what to expect from the stock repertoire of horror 'situations' but is still frightened at doors that creak, windows that are blown open by wind, creepy shadows playing on walls, cats that make sudden jumps into the frame and unholy hands that thrust from within darkness. It is the sheer unbelievability and incredulity of the ghost that so much endears it to us. In our continuing attempt to focus an interrogatory gaze on the horror genre and work towards exploring new frames of understanding it, we need to focalize on some important concepts, which are suggestive — though by no means exhaustive — in discerning the internal logic of the horror cinema.

Freud and the Uncanny

'Art-horror' is the emotional state in which works of horror or 'narratives and/or images [are] predicated upon raising the effect of horror in audiences' (Carroll, 1990, p. 15). As cultural imagination 'art-horror' allows a culture to confront what in principle is impossible for a culture to represent to itself — approximations that have no place in the culture's schematic mapping. Much of the widely accepted art-horror theory as applied to horror cinema is predicated upon the Freudian notion of the 'return of the repressed' and Julia Kristeva's notion of the 'abject' as interpreted by Barbara Creed. For Freud, the horror invokes fear of the uncanny, that affective response which arouses dreads and fears. The uncanny stems from what is known of old and long familiar, 'something which ought to remain hidden but has come to light' (Freud, 2001, p. 944). Drawing on the works of the German psychologist Ernst Jentsch and E. T. A. Hoffmann, a German author of fantastic tales, Freud elaborated that the uncanny was 'something one does not know one's way about in ... the better oriented in his environment a person is, the less readily will he get the impression of something uncanny in regard to objects and events in it (Freud, 2001, p. 931).

The uncanny springs from 'nothing new or foreign but something familiar and old established in the mind that has been estranged only by the process of repression'. The source of the uncanny feeling is connected with the phenomenon of the 'double', the constant doubling, dividing, and interchanging of the ego through mirrors and shadows.

For Freud the double was an insurance against the destruction of the ego, 'an energetic denial of the power of death', which afforded the primitive man's indulgences in unrestricted primary narcissism by dispelling the prohibition imposed upon him by the physical world. But while such idea germinated from primary narcissism, the 'double' did not disappear with the passing of the primary narcissism. Quite contrarily, it acquired new meaning from the later stages of the ego's development. Whereas repression allowed entry into civilization, the double reversed its aspect once the primary stage of animism has been surpassed and from an assurance against immortality itself becomes the 'uncanny harbinger of death' (Freud, 2001, p. 940).

Traces and residue of this primary narcissism still manifest themselves. Thus, uncanny is not something new but merely the return of the repressed, shimmering underneath the surface, ready to return at the slightest provocation. The horror films draw upon this uncanny feeling: that which is familiar yet kept out of sight: the ghost, spirit or the monster. The effect of uncanny is more easily affected when the difference between the real and the imaginary can be effaced, as through cinema. The highest degree of the uncanny is experienced in relation to the return of the dead or the undead. Thus, in Freudian terms, horror is but the return of something which has always been there in the 'Unconscious' and whose sudden appearance calls up the feeling of the familiar. The doubling effect emerges in response to the subject's crisis in confronting modernity.

Doubling, as Temenuga Trifonova reminds, was not only the effect of the rise of mass culture that stripped away every object of its individuality through mass production but was also linked intricately with national and colonial projects of the nineteenth century. Doubling became the coping mechanism through which the individual could preserve 'the privacy and unconventionality of the self' (Trifonova, 2010). Paul Coates links the 'doubling' to nineteenth century national and colonial projects, for the double appeared under two conditions, 'when other people [began] to be viewed as akin to ourselves; and when the self [was] projected into a space hitherto defined as other' (Coates, 1988, p. 32). The hold of the doubling myth in popular imagination led filmmakers like George Mêlies credited with introducing the fantastic genre, 'to experiment with cinematic effects to produce the ghostly "trace" of the double in screen' (Starks, 2002, p. 189). The double resurfaced most profoundly in the German Expressionist cinema's fascination with the repressed and the uncanny of the inter-war Weimar Republic period.

Robin Wood's Return of the Repressed

Reworking the Freudian concept of the 'return of the repressed' as understood by Marcuse and elaborated later by Gad Horowitz, Robin Wood presented an alternative model to comprehend the horror genre. Freud had put forward that humanity's movement into civilized society is marked by a 'basic repression' of inner impulses/primitive instincts which are sublimated into higher socially accepted ends. 'The essence of repression lies simply in turning something away, and keeping it at a distance, from the conscious' (Freud, 1974, p. 147). Herbert Marcuse suggested that repression operated at two levels: basic and surplus. Bound up with the ability to accept postponement of desire and its gratification, basic repression allows for the development of human beings from a seething and screaming mass of convoluted animal behaviour. For Marcuse, surplus repression is 'the result of specific societal conditions sustained in the specific interest of domination' (Marcuse, 1955, pp. 44, 81). For Foucault, repression coincided with the development of capitalism: it becomes an internal part of the bourgeois order' (Foucault, 1978, p. 5), and the dissipation of oneself in pleasure became 'incompatible with a general and intense work imperative' (Foucault, 1978, p. 6). As the hallmark of capitalist system, it both represses sexuality and orders its generalization so that 'the libido becomes concentrated in one part of the body, leaving most of the rest for use as the instrument of labour' (Savran, 1998, p. 34).

Surplus repression therefore is 'a historical formulation, the result of the subject's internalization of a specific pattern of domination' (Savran, 1998, p. 35) and guarantees the subject submission to an oppressive social order. If basic repression makes us human capable of coexistence, surplus repression fashions us as 'monogamist, heterosexual, bourgeois patriarchal capitalist' (Wood, 2003, p. 64). However, it is the insistent return of this repressed that explains various phenomena including dreams and the Freudian 'slip of the tongue'. Repression of events/memories is the ego's[1] defence mechanism, but when it is breached, the repressed emerges from the unconscious to haunt the conscious mind as the 'Other' — 'we are oppressed by something out there — a projection onto the 'Other' of what is repressed within the self. What does the 'Other' embody? How does the dominant regime of 'Representation' make us see and experience the 'Other'? First, representation is to be understood as a Foucauldian discourse, which as Stuart Hall notes, 'constructs the topic [...] governs the way that a topic can be meaningfully talked about and reasoned about ... "rules in" certain ways of talking about a topic ... "rules out", limits and restricts other ways of talking about it' (Hall, 1997, p. 44). As Foucault notes, 'it would be quite wrong to see discourse as a place where previously established objects are laid one after another like words on a page' (Foucault, 2012, p. 47). As a Foucauldian exercise representation is not a dispassionate activity, but rather a process which 'produces a self-confirming account of reality by defining an object of attention and generating concepts with which to analyze it' (Baldick, 2008, p. 92). Representation therefore is never done on a clean slate, and discourse brings in its own ideological baggage.

Second, the 'Other' represents that the bourgeois ideology cannot recognize or accept but must deal with, either through rejection and annihilation or 'by rendering and assimilating it, converting it as far as possible into a replica of itself' (Wood, 2003, p. 66). 'Otherness' defines the qualities of being different and 'Othering' becomes a process by which societies exclude 'Others'. Whereas 'Othering' may not always signify stigmatization it becomes the practice through which boundaries of self-identities are sustained and the self is defined and defended. The true thematic preoccupation of the horror genre 'is the struggle for recognition of all that our civilization represses or oppresses ... happy ending typically signifying the restoration of repression' (Wood, 2003, p. 68). With its theme of menace and destruction the horror genre has historically been regarded as articulating the historical anxieties of a nation.

Julia Kristeva and the Abject

Kristeva's definition of the abject is worth quoting at length and I will use it to anchor my own discussion on the horror narratives discussed further. Kristeva traces horror in the feelings of disgust and loathing—the affection of abjection in the subject. If Freud's uncanny account for fear, the 'abject' explains for the loathsomeness and the disgust that putrid monstrosity signifies and evokes in literary and cinematic texts. Monsters as constructed in narratives of horror are grounded in sociocultural notions of abjection and abomination: murder, incest, sexual promiscuity, bodily secretions, spilled semen, menstrual blood, and the ultimate abjection: corpse, which signifies one of the most basic forms of pollution—the body without a soul (Creed, 2002, p. 70).

The revulsion that the monstrous fiend/ghost invokes can be traced to the idea of abjection found in ancient religious and historical notions—things that were located ambiguously at the boundaries of the physical self and resisted categorization were set apart from the body as abject. According to Julia Kristeva, the abject is that which threatens to breakdown the distinction between the subject and the object or between the self and others. Through abjection, 'primitive societies marked out a precise area of their culture in order to remove it from the threatening world of animals and animalism, which were imagined as representatives of sex and murder' (Kristeva, 1982, pp. 12–13).

Following this, abjection was 'a psychological process of casting off' (Baldick, 2008, p. 1). Anything on the margins of the physical self that defied classification became abject: bodily secretions as well as, importantly, cadavers. However, if the abject threatens life it paradoxically also defines it. No matter how loathsome the abject, the subject can never fully free him/herself from it—they can only be kept at the margins and radically excluded. The abject is hence conciliated through rituals of purity after compulsory defilements as in defecation, childbirth, menstruation and the performance of last rites,[2] where the abject is engaged with through rituals and 'exorcised'. Existence is thus an everyday struggle to keep the abject excluded. Horror films evoke interstitial objects that lie at the twilight of the living and the dead, signified by abject images of blood and corpses. The undead in *Bandh Darwaza* (Closed Doors), the hand without a body in *Guest House* (Ramsay & Ramsay, 1980), the *pret atma* as a soul without a physique in *Bhoot* (The Ghost), the fantastic monster in *Dahshat* (The Terror), the amorous yet putrefied witch in *Veerana* (Wilderness), the hideous Mr. Hyde (Sanjeev Kumar) in *Chehre Pe Chehra* (Face behind Face) lying on the margins of the human self and filled with contradictions are abject because they defy taxonomical description and classification.

Thus, to define the horror film is to isolate films that work upon imparting a feeling of dread, the uncanny and the abject. The multiple-limbed fantastic beings found in pre-modern and non-Western societies despite being hybrids of human and animal do not evoke feeling of loathsomeness or disgust because the mythological discourse has located them within the discourse of the symbolic order.

Generic Codes of the Hindi Horror

The fundamental problem in defining a genre is what Andrew Tudor calls 'the empiricist dilemma' — to define a genre one must preselect a group of films for generic analysis to determine their common elements but their common element can be identified only after their analysis and not before. In other words, what should be the selection criteria for the selection process? The moment one identifies a set criteria decision has been made even before analysis! Given its pliability and malleability stemming from a range of influences, thematic concerns and distinct aesthetic modes that collide and collude with each other imparting newer generic qualities, the Hindi horror genre is marked by a conflation of aesthetic styles but nevertheless given the persistence of some of its features, we can specify some parameters with which the genre defines itself. To define the Hindi horror film genre is to first isolate films through a set of standards that distinguishes it from other films. One way to overcome the pitfalls of methodological circularity is to classify films with *a priori* judgement or assumption or common cultural consensus as to what generally constitutes a horror film. The definition of genre that emerges thus would be based on certain codes and conventions.

While Indian cinema does not compete with Hollywood directly, nonetheless, an introduction to Hollywood horror genre is not to use it as a benchmark against which to measure Hindi horror films but rather to use its divergences with the Hindi horror genre to enable a much-deeper investigation. Founding attempts of the Hollywood horror genre were directly inspired by east European folktales about blood-sucking vampires, Caribbean tales of the walking dead/zombies, and its aesthetics drives were derivatives of German Expressionism and the Victorian Gothic literature. Misha Kavka put it more succinctly when she affirms that 'the horror genre in contrast to the gothic [genre] demands that we see' (Kavka, 2002, p. 227). Working through the visual codes of haunted mansions, creaking doors, and lurking shadows, silent horror classics like Rupert Julian's *The Phantom of the Opera* (1925), James Whale's *Frankenstein* (1931) and Rouben Mamoulian's *Dr. Jekyll and Mr. Hyde* (1931) were preexisting texts which could be adapted for screen. In the early years Hollywood incorporated ecclesiastical and biblical tales, but over the decades, the horror genre has mutated leading to the creation of various subgenres that combine the horror elements with various other generic tropes of comedy, action and the thriller.

By the early 1960s, as Andrew Tudor notes, horror was tied down to 'sexuality, repression and psychosis' (Tudor, 1989, p. 47). Subsequently, ghosts and monsters were competing for onscreen diegetic space with secularized psychopaths and serial killers—Powell's *Peeping Tom* (1960), Hitchcock's *Psycho* (1960), Polanski's *Repulsion* (1965); Romero's zombies *Night of the Living Dead* (1969), and a science 'gone wrong' Neumann's *The Fly* (1958), Bernds' *Return of the Fly* (1959), Castle's *The Tingler* (1959). In these increasingly hybridized and secularized Hollywood horrors, existential battles are fought not between the good and evil but between the evil and the secular. Manifestations of evil do not exclusively hinge on the devil or demons, correspondingly the solutions that these new hybrids offer at the climax do not require divine interventions. The Bible cannot repulse Romero's zombies. The undead serial killer Jason Voorhees of *Friday the 13th* is immune to the Cross. No holy water repels Freddy Krueger in *Nightmare on the Elm Street*. In John Carpenter's *Vampires* (Carpenter, 1998) the Vatican outsources vampire hunting to a group of secular mercenaries. The unholy Mummy/Imhotep (Arnold Vosloo) in *The Mummy* (Sommers, 1999) is put to rest through a pagan not a Christian exorcism. Even the fantastical *Harry Potter* series is conspicuously marked by an absence of the church.

Witchcraft and wizardry, once condemned and punishable with death at the Inquisition have been elated to an academic subject in modern children's literature. Evil is eliminated through secular albeit violent means as in *Blade* (Norrington, 1998), *Resident Evil* (Anderson, 2002), *Underworld* (Wiseman, 2003), or alternatively evil is no longer maleficent and thus can be co-opted back into human society as in *Twilight* (Hardwicke, 2008), which presents vampires as photogenic, friendly and sexy. Evil's definition has also undergone a revision; evil is no longer monstrous, malevolent and life threatening. Blade (Wesley Snipes), the vampire killer, is half vampire. Hellboy in *Hellboy* (Toro, 2004) is but a demon delivered through Hell's portal. Van Abraham Helsing (Hugh Jackman) the famed Dutch vampire hunter in *Van Helsing* (Sommers, 2004) is a werewolf himself but no longer evil. The eponymous demon hunter John Constantine (Keanu Reeves) in *Constantine* (Lawrence, 2005) who sends back demons to hell knows that he is destined to return there on his death. Lacking a Gothic literary tradition, Hindi horror cinema has borrowed significantly from Hindu traditional folk beliefs. And with zombies ambling across Indian silver screens as late as 2013 with *Go Goa Gone* (Nidimoru & Krishna, 2013) the Hindi horror cinema normatively presents spirits/ghosts of dead people who come back to wreck vengeance and are operationalized through a permutation and combination of denied last rites, and ancient curses that can lay dormant for centuries and still remain potent within the modern Nehruvian secular discourse.

Conjunctions and Departures with Hollywood

Central to our understanding of the Hindi horror genre is the recognition that its heritage is marked by heterogeneity of inputs, influences and developments. If it has borrowed its aesthetics from the German Expressionism early on it has also maintained a faithful contiguity with the generic formulations of Hollywood, the Italian *Giallo* and lately the Thai, Japanese, and Korean horror. From the hard to miss camera aesthetics of distorted angles, baroque interiors, chiaroscuro, spot lighting, and surrealistic settings of *Mahal* (The Palace) (Amrohi, 1949), and *Madhumati* (Roy, 1958), to the unrestrained amateur filmmaking aesthetics and 'found footage' shaky hand-held camera videotape in *Question Mark* (Patel & Dave, 2012) and *Six Minus Five Equals Two* (Jain, 2014); from the culturally alien monstrosities like the walking dead in *Do Gaz Zameen Ke Neechay* (Beneath Two Feet of Earth) (Ramsay, 1972), the virgin-brides murdering wolfman in *Jaani Dushman* (Mortal Enemy) (Kohli, 1979), a weretiger in *Junoon* (Obsession) (Bhatt, 1992), a killer doll in *Paapi Gudia* (Sinful Doll) (D'Souza, 1996), the vampire in *Wohi Bhayanak Raat* (That Frightful Night) (Talwar, 1989), a grossly bandaged Mummy in *Dak Bangla* (Guest House) (Ramsay, 1987), the hideous winged creature monster of *Jeepers Creepers* (Salva, 2001) in *Kaalo* (Louis, 2010), the pale faced darkly eye shadowed ghosts of *The Grudge* and *Juon* (Shimizu, 2002; Shimizu, 2004) in *Vaastu Shastra* (Narang, 2004), the too obvious Caucasian zombies on the rampage after a drug overdose in *Go, Goa ,Gone* (Nidimoru & Krishna, 2013) the Hindi horror genre has used Hollywood horror as an extensive point of derivation.

With the coming of the Ramsays, the deployment of modern regime of special effects of the prosthetics made it easier to present explicit representation of the bizarre, the gruesome and the outright grotesque. Hindi horror films combined varied visual elements of colour filters, panoramic shots, mobile subjective camera gaze, horse-drawn carriages, haunted *haveli*, cavities behind walls, trap doors, creepy paintings, ancient curses that remain potent across generations, mad vagrants 'who seem to know', and other Gothic trappings drawn from the Hammer Productions; gratuitous nudity and grotesque prosthetic elements drawn from the Italian Giallo and the slasher genre, interspersed with digressive subplots of comedy and action. Even the supernatural monster in *Darwaza* (The Doors) (Ramsay & Ramsay, 1978) was designed by 'legendary British makeup artist Christopher Tucker, and inspired by the hunchback of Notre Dame' (Majumder, 2012). A severed hand on a postmortem murderous rampage in *The Beast with Five Fingers* (Florey, 1946), and *Now the Screaming Starts* (Baker, 1973) appears as a prominent influence and a clear inspiration for the Ramsays' *Guest House* (Ramsay & Ramsay, 1980). *Bandh Darwaza* (Ramsay & Ramsay, 1990) reimagines Dracula as Neola even as the reworking of the narrative transplants the vampire from Transylvania to the hinterland of the Western *Ghats* of Maharashtra as he haunts *Kali Pahadi* at night, his libidinal excess apparent as he plunges his fangs into bare female necks reminiscent of Christopher Lee's rendition of the Count Dracula in countless Hammer Productions. *Gehrayee* (The Depth) and *Jadu Tona* (Black Magic) render tales of possessed pubescent females. S. U. Sayed's *Saat Saal Baad* (Seven Years Later) (Sayed, 1989) bears out *Friday the 13th* as a mysterious murderer goes on a rampage; the camera often capturing the victim through the point of view of the killer.

Mahakaal (The Monster) (Ramsay & Ramsay, 1993) references A *Nightmare on the Elm Street* (Craven, 1984) as it introduces Shakaal, complete with a burnt face and armed with razor-fitted glove to kill his victims in their dreams (Figure 2.1). *Shaitani Ilaaka* (Devil's Domain) (Ramsay, 1990) features a sequence where a possessed hand tries to kill its 'owner' much like Ash William's (Bruce Campbell) in Sam Raimi's cult classic *Evil Dead II: Dead by Dawn* (Raimi, 1987). A possessed Smriti/Sangeeta (Tia Bajpai) in *1920: The Evil Returns* (Patel B. , 2012) can contort her body upside down like Linda Styles (Julie Carmen) in *In the Mouth of Madness* (Carpenter, 1994). *Fright Night* (Holland, 1985) becomes *Wohi Bhayanak Raat* (Talwar, 1989). And if *Raaz* (The Secret) (Bhatt, 2002) shares major narrative trajectory of *What Lies Beneath* (Zemeckis, 2000), then *Hawa* (The Wind) (Dhanoa, 2003) reiterates *The Entity* (Furie, 1982) about a single woman who is tormented and sexually molested by an evil spirit.

Figure 2.1: The culturally alien monstrosity with razor-fitted glove in *Mahakaal* draws its inspiration from *A Nightmare on Elm Street*.
Courtesy: Ramsay Productions.

Mumbai 125 KM (Madhukar, 2014) retells *Dead End* (Jean-Baptiste & Canepa, 2003). Since the 2000s, Hindi horror cinema has turned its gaze eastwards for generic stimulations. *Naina* (The Eyes) (Morakhia, 2005) recreates Pang Brothers sleeper hit horror film *The Eye* (Phat & Chun, 2002), just as *Click* (Sivan, 2010) pledges by its Thai original *Shutter* (Espiritos–A Morte Estáao Seu Lado) (Pisanthanakun & Wongpoom, 2004). *Alone* (Patel, 2015) is another remake of *Alone* (Pisanthanakun & Wongpoom, 2007).

In detailing these generic convergences, it is certainly not to aver that each Hindi cinema's horror moment is only an exercise in bootlegging, for it runs the risk of flattening out the complexities of a genre's innovative variations. To view every generic attempt at horror in terms of 'copy' ignores the ideological subversion that the original is often subjected to, for every attempt at reconfiguration of an original entails a mix of pastiches, parody, parallel tracks of comedy and love stories that make them uniquely sophisticated and mark their departure from the archetype. Further, it is inconceivable for generic films to maintain clinical detachment and vestality from similarly organized generic attempts as various Hollywood re-rendering of Thai or Japanese horror will testify.

I am tempted to quote Bakhtin, who puts it, 'when we select words in the process of constructing utterances … we usually take them from other utterances and mainly from utterances that are kindred to ours in *genre* that is in theme, composition or style' (Bakhtin, 1986, p. 86). As *Bakhtinian* utterances, generic attempts are pastiches and never themselves originary. [They are] 'always an answer to another utterance that precede[d] it and [are] therefore always conditioned by, and in turn qualif[y] the prior utterance to a greater or lesser degree' (Holquist, 2010, p. 60).

Whereas certain aesthetic or thematic styles are easy to recognize, other rhetorical instances of the Hindi horror genre have been more subtle. Much like Bakhtian 'utterances' the Hindi horror genre has taken other utterances and what has emerged in the Hindi horror genre from these two distinct voices is a vampire who is repulsed by the Hindu 'Om' and the Muslim Koran as in *Bandh Darwaza* (Ramsay & Ramsay, 1990), werewolf/wolfman who dies only when pierced by consecrated *trishuls* (tridents) as in *Jaani Dushman* and *Darwaza*; necromancer who is tormented when left in the precinct of hallowed ground of a Hindu temple and liquefies when exposed to the divine gaze of Lord Shiva as in *Veerana*; a Mummy which erupts in spontaneous combustion when exposed to *Surya Devta* (sun) as in *Dak Bangla* (Ramsay, 1987); an indigenized Freddy Keueger who can be repelled by consecrated amulet as in *Mahakaal* and a witch whose lair in the underworld can be reached through an apartment's escalator by pressing the 666 as in *Ek Thi Daayan* (There Was Once a Witch) (Iyer, 2013).

Violence shorn of celestial sanction is rarely effective. It must be consecrated by divinity. The monstrous evil in the Hindi horror genre is linked to faith in a way that American horror is not. Far more steeped in tradition than science, 'there has been no "Its' alive" moment in the Hindi horror genre' (Mubarki, 2013, p. 43). There are very few corporeal monsters. The Hindi horror genre normatively deals with the supernatural and has a monster with a more ethereal form: evil spirit or *pret atma* which essentializes its narratives. The return of the dead to the world of the living remains a contact element even if the terms and features of the 'return' have changed over the years. For Hindu scriptural texts, death is liberating for the soul, as it frees the spirit from its worldly bondage and laws: both temporal and physical. This exemption from Newtonian physics reawakens their inherent orphic powers, unearthly abilities and imparts them with abilities such as those of virtual invisibility, omniscience, and superhuman strength, endowing them with the power to inflict pain and punishment on others. And unlike the Semitic ethos of Christianity and Islam with their personification of Evil through the Devil or the *Iblis/Shaitaan*, Hindu mythology has no such counterparts. Evil in Hindi horror genre is much less ambitious, with no plans for worldly domination and rarely ventures out beyond the domain of the immediate, unlike say the anti-Christ in *The Omen* (Donner, 1976), *End of Days* (Hyams, 1999) or the horror hack writer Sutter Cane (Jürgen Prochnow) in *In the Mouth of Madness* (Carpenter, 1994). The monster/ghost/evil in Hindi horror genre does not threaten us; excuse the inadvertent pun, with the 'end of days' or a 'war of the worlds'.

The intended purpose of horror is to 'characteristically or ideally promote horror; this emotion constitutes the identifying mark of horror' (Carroll, 1990, p. 14). The reaction of fear, dread and disgust by the characters to the ghost within the diegetic narration acts as a normative cue to the audiences to react similarly. The monster/ghost/spirit disrupts our sense of present/past, ancient/modern. By its very nature, the ghost/monster/spirit/*atma* is an abject object stretched along between the two realms of the living and the dead. In its corporeal manifestation as a monster with rotten putrefying mass of seething flesh, it invokes as much disgust as fear as screen characters often recoil, shrink and withdraw from its profane touch. The feeling of disgust becomes auxiliary to the evocation of fear and dread. These affective responses expressed within the narration essentialize the Hindi horror film. Films with ghosts such as *Chamatkar* (Miracle) (Mehra, 1992), *Maa* (Mother) (Kashyap, 1992), *Hello Brother* (Khan, 1999), *Paheli* (The Riddle) (Palekar, 2005), *Bhootnath* (Lord of Ghosts) (Sharma, 2008), *Hum Tum Aur Ghost* (Me, You and Ghost) (Kaushik, 2010), *Bhootnath Returns* (Tiwari, 2014), *Gang of Ghosts* (Kaushik, 2014) or with monsters such as *Koi Mil Gaya* (Found Someone) (Roshan, 2003), *Ra.One* (Sinha, 2011) or *Krrish 3* (Roshan, 2013) are not horror films since they arouse mirth and sympathy and there is little attempt to invoke fear, dread or disgust, the staple emotive reactions that the horror genre seeks to arouse.

Generic Features of the Hindi Horror

Note that my intention here is not to present the horror genre
in all its cinematic possibilities, but given how relatively constant some of its features are we can specify the general, not
absolute contours by which Hindi horror films can be identified as primarily or substantially horror, though this may
not work for films of the 1960s such as *Mahal*, *Madhumati*,
Kohraa (The Fog), etc. Generically, most Hindi horror films
present an idyllic peaceful situation which is breached by
an unnatural death — either suicide or murder, leading to a
satanic intrusion that initially goes unrecognized. Because
of 'unbelief' and general apathy and scepticism towards
everything spiritual, ghosts go 'unacknowledged' and the
supernatural hypothesis is initially rejected. Only when
no rational account explains the bodies that keep piling
up, the possession thesis is accepted. Even here, the principal protagonist/s often resort to science and reason and
apply secular restorative methods that inevitably end in
debacle. Violence, so potent in the Hollywood horror genre,
is usually ineffective, unless sanctified by divinity. These
discoveries equip the principle protagonist and prime the
audience for the denouement. Therefore, a general recognition of traditional, tralatitious spirituality by the principal
characters must come first before any meaningful 'skirmish'
with evil can take place. Reassertion of traditional–cultural
values is the first step in countering evil. In their narrative
closures, the normative reasserts itself over the empirical,
the ancient over the modern, and the traditional carves out
the domain of the spiritual, wherefrom modernity has been
banished altogether. The climax of Hindi horror films often
employs religious sacraments and appurtenances to defeat
supernatural evil forces. Therefore, despite belonging to the
horror genre, horror films often deal with faith and belief
like mythological films. A 'return to faith' marks the centrality of the Hindi horror genre and becomes the basis for

its generic contours being different from the Hollywood horror genre. It also marks the horror genre's affinity with the Hindu mythologicals for its subversion of the known laws of space–time and for the way in which divinities in mythological and ghosts in horror cinema defy rational logic, laws of corporeal reality and realize impossible onto-logical experiences. These codes and conventions in varying permutations and combinations impart the unity of a genre to Hindi horror cinema.

Horror Cinema as Project of/for the 'Nation'

Whereas Hindi horror films have certain broad ideological tendencies that have been earmarked for the later chapters that make up the primary conversation of this book, an enquiry into wider genealogy of post-colonial Hindi cinema and its inherent themes will set up the basis from which to establish the horror genre's ideological framework.

Post-colonial Bombay cinema produced a seamless nation where traumatic ruptures like the abject moment of Partition and the communal holocaust were made inconspicuous, and cinema came to be looked upon as an apparatus with a potentially integrative function. It could absorb the vari-ous undercurrents of extant sub-nationalism. If filmmak-ers obviated the trauma of partition in popular cinema, it could evade authorial intention and intrude into narratives that often hinged on cinematic discourses of family separa-tion and reunions. Post-Independence Hindi cinema had to exercise 'monumental repression of denial and disavowal of communal politics, presenting an idyllic oneness, unity among undifferentiated Indians' (Virdi, 2003, p. 73). The government's institution of the Best Feature Film on National Integration in 1966 with the explicit aim of promoting 'social cohesion and national consolidation' (Benegal, 2007, p. 231) not only underscored the fear of another partition etched into the national psyche but also underlined the optimism that Hindi cinema being the commonest cultural indulgences of Indians could create a homogenized idea of Indian nationhood.

In its own aesthetic ways, Hindi cinema also persistently responded to national crises. Wars with China and Pakistan in the mid-1960s created a new wave of patriotic and spy thrillers like *Haqeeqat* (The Reality) (Anand, 1964), *Shaheed* (The Martyr) (Sharma, 1965), *Himalay Ki Godmein* (In the Lap of the Himalayas) (Bhatt, 1965), *Upkaar* (Benevolence) (Kumar, 1967), *Farz* (Duty) (Nagaich, 1967), *Aakhen* (Eyes) (Sagar, 1968), *Saat Hindustani* (Seven Indians) (Abbas, 1969), *Purab Aur Paschim* (East and West) (Kumar, 1970), *Lalkar* (Challenge) (Sagar, 1972), *Hindustan Ki Kasam* (India's Oath) (Anand, 1973), etc.

To offset accusations of majoritarianism, Nehruvian secular ideals created 'cultural enclaves' or socio-temporal space that granted autonomy to ethnic and religious minorities. And pluralistic Nehruvianism came to be understood as 'non-sectarianism in the public sphere', embracing a spectrum of political opinions, ranging from socialism and secularism to scientific rationalism and aligned against conservative Hindu orthodoxy, seeking the submission of the sacred/spiritual to the secular/temporal as exemplified by Hindi films *Mahal* (Amrohi, 1949) and *Madhumati* (Roy, 1958) the initiatory address of post-Independence Hindi horror cinema.

Nevertheless, 'where there is power there is resistance' (Foucault, 1979, p. 95). This hegemonic Nehruvian rationalist secularism espousing a range of calibrated modernist discourses did not go unchallenged and engendered counter-narratives. Post-Emergency India saw the development of several significant social discourses, among them the return of the traditional discourses with a strong undercurrent of majoritarian Hindutva. These perspectives became especially important in relation to the genre of horror seeking to produce a world of myths, miracles legends. In the 1970s, the cultural–traditional backlash drawing its energies from a variety of counter-narratives castigated scientific rationalism as in *Jadu Tona* (Nagaich, 1977), and *Gehrayee* (Raje & Desai, 1980). On the other hand, *Chehre Pe Chehra* (Tilak, 1981) and *Dahshat* (Ramsay & Ramsay, 1981) as 'moral tales of scientific excesses' marked a frontal encounter between the mythic and the empirical succinctly dramatizing science's troubled place in the post-colonial Indian condition. Another subgenre, the 'monstrous "other" feminine' narratives of *Mangalsutra* (Nupital Necklace) (Vijay, 1981) and *Veerana* (Ramsay & Ramsay, 1988), produced in the 1980s deified and reinforced traditional gendered perspectives, where perverse female sexuality commanding sovereign female desire and controlling gaze, is annihilated, and normative patriarchal order is restored.

Commencing from around the mid-1980s a series of violent ethnic separatist movements presented existential threats that seriously imperiled the viability of the Indian State. A state system under siege brought forth the view that the causal agency of these 'separatist outbursts' ostensibly orchestrated by Indian religious minorities was located in the autonomous 'separate' cultural space created for them through constitutionally guaranteed cultural rights, actively promoted by the secular and pluralistic ethos of the Nehru era which prevented their integration into the 'mainstream'. While the traditional backlash witnessed in the late 1970s was culturally neutral and inclusive since it pitted science and secularism against faith and belief in general, this was to change in view of the specificities of the ethnic onslaught that the Indian State was subjected to in the post-Emergency period. Cultural neutrality subsequently gave way to effervescent sectarian Hindutva by the early 1990s.

A balance of payment crisis led the Congress government to initiate economic reforms leading to the opening up of Indian markets to international competition and sparked off economic and cultural anxieties about an imminent sweep of Westernization. The film industry lend itself to this emerging cultural nationalism through the construction of Hindi (melo)dramas which presented 'a remarkably consistent pattern in producing a monolith Indian identity that [was] Hindu, wealthy and patriarchal' (Malhotra & Alagh, 2004, p. 19). Whereas *Jadu Tona* (Nagaich, 1977) and *Gehrayee* (Raje & Desai, 1980) critiqued transformative modernity and urbanization, Hindi horror narratives in the post-Hindutva mobilization era like *1920* (Bhatt, 2008) and *Haunted* (Bhatt, 2011) as speculative stance of the Hindutva ideologic position are relatively novel phenomena and narratives that critique both Nehruvian pluralist ethos and scientific rationalism.

The long discursive terrain of the horror genre reveals linear temporal development combined with cyclic ones. The films have been chosen for a number of reasons. *Mahal* (Amrohi, 1949) and *Madhumati* (Roy, 1958) as the foundational horror moments of the Hindi cinema are the prototypical examples of the Nehruvian secular rationalism as they seek the submission of the spiritual to the temporal. Their aesthetic and thematic tropes became templates for the later Hindi horror films. *Jadu Tona* (Nagaich, 1977) and *Gehrayee* (Raje & Desai, 1980) while carrying the stamp of inclusivity, as we shall see, are celebratory of folk traditions' potency in countering evil even as they seek to 'other' modernity and thus mark a momentous break in the genre. Their theme signifies a general disillusionment with the secular/temporal line of *Mahal* and *Madhumati* even while they attempt to stem the subversion of the spiritual by a 'dystopic' modernity.

1920 (Bhatt, 2008) and *Haunted* (Bhatt, 2011) attempt the absorption of all oppositional elements and uses modernity as a means of sustaining traditionalism for the new Hindutva social order. The mechanics of the Hindutva ideologic hinges on cultural exclusivity and the imputation of 'Hinduness'.

Much like the spy and thriller genre, the Hindi horror cinema and its mutating subgenres have also responded by representing key moments of social history in their modes of address through allegorization: the triumph of Nehruvian secularism in *Mahal* and *Madhumati* (Roy, 1958), the backlash of traditional culturalism in *Jadu Tona* and *Gehrayee, Chehre Pe Chehra* and *Dahshat;* the deification of an imperiled patriarchy and reiteration of gendered relations shaken under Nehruvian era through the monstrous 'other' narratives of *Mangalsutra, Raaz* and *Suryavanshi;* the polemics of Hindutva through *1920* and *Haunted* (Bhatt, 2011). These films should not be seen as examples but rather as opportunities to think what a given film proposes and exemplifies. Through analyses of the select films, this book will attempt a preliminary explication of the discursive strategies and semiotic sleight of hands employed to connect their ideological orientations and cinematic resolutions.

The Hindi horror genre like other genres revolves exclusively around the concerns of the majority Hindu community because their struggles are presumed to be both appealing and universally accessible to all audiences. Exorcisms are performed mostly through Hindu rituals, and while the engagement of the sacraments of minority Indian religious communities is a rarity, the genre has avoided creating 'narrative spaces' where different faiths get to 'fight it out' among themselves. The benign potency of other faiths is skilfully acknowledged, by positioning the narrative text of Hindi horror films as a dyad contest between an 'unbelieving' secular science and spiritual traditionalism/folk traditions. Hinduism, thus appropriates the space meant for the latter and speaks for all the faiths 'absent' in the diegetic narrative. Hindi horror cinema thus lies at the intersections of myth, ideology, and dominant socioreligious thought and deals with religious themes. Historical and cultural anxieties often animate ghosts in the Hindi horror. If the ghost during the Nehruvian milieu go away on its own and needs no 'exorcism' as in *Madhumati* (Roy, 1958), in *1920* (Bhatt, 2008), it has to be actively expelled through explicit

Hindu rituals. Through its instrumentalities the horror genre presents a space in which the nation is made, unmade and remade in popular imagination.

Nature of the Hindi Horror Genre

The Hindi horror genre is a representational space for ideational struggle and juxtapose the tralatitious order and the modernist discourse as the two opposite discursive premises in the genre's thematic binary opposites, setting the stage for conflict between the normative/empirical, the ancient/modern, the secular/traditional, and the rational/ spiritual order which permits a heteroglotic representation of conflicting worldviews and imaginations of the Indian nation-state. Whereas the word tralatitious means 'handed-down', to serve my purpose I define it as non-monolithic and operationally plural quotidian cultural practices that the secular order seeks to reverse, demean, and or annul from the everyday. The tralatitious order haunts the edge of the secular order as an indeterminate menace and potential violation of its established rational norms. It is a negation of the certainty and solidity of the secular rational world, the opening up of indefinite possibilities of existence. The world of the spirits as imagined cinematically has appeared cooperative/conciliative at some instances and competitive/militant at other times in its struggle with Nehruvian secularism over the definition of Indianess, secularism and modernity, and representation of femininity and the Hindutva. In its narrative operations the Hindi horror genre is indissolubly wedded into ideological contests.

This book attempts to situate the subtext of the ideological contests framed by cinematography and establish linkages between the filmic world and broad social and historical formations. The Hindi horror genre presents a fertile territory for inviting intrusive practices of interpretations, and I shall add here that since the ideological anchorages can be located in the climax, an examination of the 'climactic solutions' offered by the genre along with thematic interrogation reveals three major strands with varying forms of narration and style: the secular conscious, the traditional–cultural, and the *Hindutva* ideologic, each corresponding to the way the nation has been imagined at various times. Thematically organized cluster of films, each corresponding to the subgenre offers the advantage of chalking out each phase of the genre, sanctioning us to develop a genre analysis, look for tectonic shifts within individual films and mark the evolution of the genre and its transmutation into strands of subgenres.

An interrogation of these strands, which have developed at the intersections of cultural politics and political transformations, will allow us not only to articulate the Hindi horror genre and its subsets but also to mark their ideological positions. Any adequate structural analysis must take into account not only the deep underlying edifice but also consider the way in which the mise-en-scene, individual shots and camera movements reflect the internal logic of the genre. The effort is to contextualize interpretations and reexamine them in their historically specific moments of production and consumption. Interpretations, when grounded in historical struggles and not to the essence of films make the context of the film as important as the text: the rituals of aesthetics become a tool for marking ideological positions. The perceived meaning of a film must not be tied to the specific text alone but examine the social motivations and expectations that oversaw its production. To understand the promulgated meaning one must comprehend the ways in which films have interacted with and resonated within larger social constellations. Meaning is produced at the intersection of genre expectation, the spectators' field of experience and the dominant social and political milieu. Any dissection of spectatorship qualifies itself with the rider that, 'no physiological sensors or strategic interviews or questionnaire results can ever tell the whole story about a matter as complicated and idiosyncratic as how spectators interact with a film' (Lowenstein, 2010, p. 120).

A word of caution: All (re)interpretations offer only a horizon of possibilities and can never tell the 'whole story' since the production of meaning for and by the spectator is always in excess of its intention. This book tries to bridge the gap that currently exists in the field. Disagreements if any should serve to open the debate rather than restrict it. *Mahal, Madhumati* or *Woh Kaun Thi?* (Who Was She?) may not qualify as a copybook instance of a horror film going by the generic instances of horror films of the 1980s and the 1990s with their grotesque prosthetics and have been defined as horror only retrospectively. But as Mark Jankovich succinctly notes that films like the *Phantom of the Opera* (Julian, 1925), *House of Dracula* (Kenton, 1945), *The Return of the Vampire* (Landers, 1944), *Curse of the Cat People* (Wise & Fritsch, 1944) and *The Isle of the Dead* (Robson, 1945) have also been retrospectively labelled as horror and at the time of their release were deemed thrillers (Jancovich, 2009). Indeed, many Hollywood films of the 1940s now 'understood' as horror films were identified as thrillers at the times of their release. And here I posit that the Hindi horror genre has in fact evolved from the Gothic narrations of the unseen that evoke fear of the Unknown (*Madhumati, Woh Kaun Thi? Kohraa, Bees Saal Baad*) to films that appeal outright to the feelings of fear, dread and disgust, and revulsion (disfigured faces, disintegrating bodies, in *Darwaza, Jaani Dushman, Guest House, Chehre Pe Chehra, Dahshat, Hotel, Mangalsutra, Purana Mandir, Saamri, Tahkhana*, etc.). Popular generic cinema draws its 'topics, treatments, agendas, personnel, images of the audiences, [and] definition of the situation from [...] wider sociocultural and political structures of which they are a differentiated part' (Hall, 1980, p. 129) and the post-colonial epoch has engendered subgenres that reflects particular paramount sociocultural obsessions—the secularism of the Nehruvian era—the rebellious anti-establishment return of the conservative narratives of the post-Emergency period and the Hindu polemics of the post-liberalization India to which I shall now turn.

Notes

1. Freud described the ego as the 'coherent organization of mental processes' (Freud, 1960 [1923], pp. 5–6).
2. In Eastern cultures, menstrual blood defiles the body, and the woman must undertake a ritual bath before entering the prayer chamber or the family kitchen. Islamic traditions prohibit sexual intercourse with spouse when she is menstruating. See Chapter 2 Verse 222. Likewise in normative Hindu cultural practices touching the dead body is considered defilement. In Islamic tradition, the dead are given *ghusl*, a ritual cleansing bath, before burial.

3

Secular Conscious Narrative

After Independence, given the needs of a post-colonial society seeking to meet the challenges of modernity with a new, secular, scientific, social order, the modernizing state sought to suppress the primordial, the traditional, and the orthodox. What this secular, scientific, social order could not accept or recognize was either repressed or rendered safe through absorption. This chapter seeks to explore secular Indian consciousness as a political idea and the way Hindi horror cinema has 'observed' and 'reflected' this as a *filmic* concept.

Given the presence of monstrosities, the horror genre is as Sangita Gopal notes 'particularly suited to expressing historical shifts including those pertaining to cinematic form and technology since it is entrusted with producing the norm and its disruption' (Gopal, 2011, p. 92). To map the trajectories and the sub-mutations of the Hindi horror genre it is pertinent to understand what the genre has drawn upon and what it has distanced itself from. To understand secularism is to understand modernity which emphasizes empirical evidence over normative beliefs. Modernity functions on the generalizability of knowledge and a belief in the susceptibility of knowledge to certainty and provability; truth can be established only through its demonstrability and ascertainability. This modernity can establish itself only through an engagement with the 'Other'. Like Capitalism, modernity seeks expansion and exhibits homogenizing tendencies. This is what makes modernity exclusive.

Subjects that eschew certainty and provability stand outside the periphery and command no engagement with modernity. As the most visible facet of modernity, secularism is 'a process of differentiation which results in the various aspects of society, economic, political, legal and moral becoming increasingly discrete in relation to each other' (Srinivas, 1984). The very actualization, even if partial of the secular, 'involves not only a rejection of the religious-cultural patterns of life of that society but also a systematic attempt to overturn the status-quo' (Alam, 1999, p. 4). Since ancient and spiritual truths like matters of faith and belief cannot indubitably be proved through demonstrability and ascertainability, they stand rejected. A natural corollary to secularism is rationalism, or 'the prevalence of a scientific temper, a rationalization of worldview of the individual, and the reduction of religious belief to affect' (Srivastava, 2008, p. 18), with the avowed aim to regulate social life in accordance with the principles of reason and in a Freudian sense to *eliminate* or *to banish* to the background everything irrational from the conscious. This rationalist secularism formed the basis of state secularism in post-Independence India, and the traditional–cultural mode of expression was repressed into a cultural unconsciousness.

Secularism in the Indian Context

While acknowledging the limitations of science and reason in a society where traditionalism sanctioned social and quotidian conducts, the founding fathers of the Indian Republic consented, not without dissent and scepticism, that the new emerging post-colonial India must make a break from its past, and old traditional ideas must either be reworked into newly formed democratic order or abandoned. Thus, the historical precedents of being a land of refuge to persecuted communities became instances of magnanimous toleration and absorption of divergent ways of life which were to be accommodated and formally sanctified through communally neutral practices of the state.

Organized religions had allied themselves with entrenched casteist and communal interests and split the nationalist movement along sectarian lines leading to the partition. They threatened to keep in abeyance the guaranteed individual rights that paternal constitutionalism wanted to offer to its subject citizenry. Therefore, acts of imperial magnanimity under Asoka and Akbar became the alibi for modern statecraft offering justifications for keeping the 'church' and the 'state' separate, even though there were plenty of historical instances to the contrary.

Scientific temper, if not science itself, became the antidote of organized religion. As Nehru put it, 'scientific approach and temper are or should be, a way of life, a process of thinking' (Nehru, 2004, p. 570). Religion must necessarily shrink as knowledge expands. Science, therefore, was but an act of dissent against the dominant discourse of social and religious orthodoxy much like the way the Indian nationalist movement was the counternarrative to the discourse of Imperialism. But did this require a complete dissociation from the past? Nehru's faith in rationalism did not discount the possibility that 'the scientific method of observation [may] not always be applicable to the varieties of human experiences' (Nehru, 2004, p. 570). Well aware of what a carte blanche to science had done and was doing to Europe, which periodically indulged in colossal acts of self-destruction, Nehru's secularism and scientism did not envisage a complete and final breach between faith and belief. Instead he noted that 'when both science and philosophy fail us, we shall have to rely on other such powers of apprehension as we may possess' (Nehru, 2004, p. 570). This succinctly envisaged an intervening role for the state: wielding science and secularism for one set of occasions and faith and dogma for another.

The move to introduce reformist intrusions upon classical Hinduism through legislation was thus guided by these motives and was not without opposition from traditional quarters within the Congress itself. But even while recognizing the limits of such an approach Nehru had retrospectively made his intentions clear well in advance from within the four walls of Ahmadnagar Fort in 1944:

> Even when we go to the regions beyond the reach of the scientific method and visit the mountains tops where philosophy dwells and the high emotions [such as beauty and charm] fill us ... that approach and temper [the scientific method of objective inquiry] are still necessary. (Nehru, 2004, p. 571)

As Nehru put it in his inimitable tongue-in-cheek style, 'even if God exists, it may be desirable not to look up to Him, or to rely upon Him' (Nehru, 2004, p. 571). Under Nehru, secularism was combined with the developmentalist approach, in the hope that 'large-scale application of science would overcome the possibility of major societal upheaval' (Bhaneja, 1976, p. 99). Economic and social development would offset violent revolutionary tendencies that frightened Indian bourgeoisie; secularism became a state-sponsored project and Nehruvian secularism became 'the consensus that undergirded the Indian developmental state, referring to a particular distribution of political power and its legitimating vision of secular, autarkic growth (Rajagopal, 2001, p. 32).

Since 'the western discourse on modernity is a shifting, hybrid configuration consisting of different, often conflicting theories, norms, historical experiences, utopian fantasies and ideological commitments' (Gaonkar, 2001, p. 15), privileging a particular approach specially the national/cultural construct of interrogation to explore this modernity will allow us to understand its operations within cultural specificities. It will allow us to show how *Jadu Tona* (Nagaich, 1977) and *Gehrayee* (Raje & Desai, 1980) reconfigure modernity and challenge the consensus on Indian secularism. Similarly, situating the monstrous 'other' feminine narratives in other 'theatres of modernity' (Gaonkar, 2001, p. 16) will allow us to interrogate the discourse of patriarchy threatened by the imperatives of secular modernity and probe the anti-science discourse through the visual registers of *Dahshat* (Ramsay & Ramsay, 1981) and *Chehre Pe Chehra* (Tilak, 1981).

An overwhelming desire in favour of 'social reforms' accorded legitimacy to intrusive state actions and the Hindi horror genre can be unravelled most productively within the discursive strategies of this interface between culture and modernity; the undercurrents of the horror genre can be best understood in terms of the mechanics of cultural modernization. What this secular, scientific and social order could not accept or recognize was either repressed or rendered safe through absorption. This is precisely what the 'return of the repressed' narrative of the Hindi horror genre articulates in *Mahal* (Amrohi, 1949) and later *Madhumati* (Roy, 1958). With its theme of the supernatural, *Mahal*, *Madhumati* and *Kohraa* (Nag, 1964) draw upon the German expressionistic mode of melodrama and exhibit an intensity of expression through slow and deliberate narrative pace overly emphatic visual style.

Mahal: The Inaugural Moment of the Secular Consciousness

Disdain for the spiritual distinguishes the narration of *Mahal*, arguably India's first post-Independence horror film. *Mahal's* narrative and aesthetic conventions and its pioneering visual and aural symbolism derived from the Expressionist movement distinguish it as the inaugural moment of the post-Independence horror genre. The aesthetic tropes of distorted camera angles, exaggerated perspectives, Gothic mise-en-scene and dark silhouettes creating an ambience of fear and dread became the template of the genre to be used by the later Hindi horror films.

The Expressionist movement flourished during Germany's Weimar period specifically because of preceding period of import ban between 1916 and 1920, which allowed the German cinema to prosper in the absence of competition. German Expressionist movement was a reflection of a national psyche: national humiliation through a tragic war which had been brought to an end under equally mortifying conditions. The revolutionary Expressionistic style was an attempt to bring 'the unconscious to the fore, to the level of consciousness where malaise and hysteria can be expressed' (Hayward, 1996, p. 192). The 1940s was the period when many foreign technicians and artists came down to work in India often bringing in their superior technical skills, among them Josef Wirsching, a cinematographer born in Germany in 1903 who had studied photography theory in Munich. Before moving to India, Wirsching had worked on a spate of German films, and his illustrious career saw him work as a camera assistant and lab assistant before moving up the hierarchy to handle the camera as the director of photography for Himanshu Rai's *Bombay Talkies*. His lighting techniques and the camera works imparted an impeccable touch of German Expressionism to the mise-en-scene of *Mahal* (Figure 3.1). The camera's disoriented frame often collecting darkness at the corners, the uneven lighting of objects became the mode of portraying the inner turmoil and anguish of characters. It was the camera's attempt to capture Freud's unconscious mind, seeking to bring to the fore, repressed human emotions of pain, anguish and trauma. Through a show of exaggerated shadows, high contrast, disorienting set designs, distorted camera angles, a ruined palace long forgotten, silhouettes framed against lighter background which gave an aura of spectral presence

Figure 3.1: The interplay of light and shadow on the edges of the frame impart mystical elements to Kamini (Madhubala) in *Mahal*.
Courtesy: Bombay Talkies Ltd.

to dimly lit scenes, *Mahal* anticipated the aesthetics of films such as *Madhumati, Bees Saal Baad* (After Twenty Years) and *Woh Kaun Thi?*

Reminiscent of *The Cabinet of Dr. Caligari* (Wiene, 1920), lighting in *Mahal* controls the line of sight and directs the audiences to concentrate on certain parts of the frame, and through spotlighting a character is lit and not the whole frame, leaving the rest to darkness. With its *noirish* style of single-point candles, flickering shadows, sparse editing, silhouettes, oblique camera angles, and camera frames often foregrounded over architectural patterns, the arches and the columns in *Mahal* (Figure 3.2) create an intricate pattern that portends the gloomy atmospherics of the film's theme of death and reincarnation. The complex architectural composition allowed for an intricate play of light and shadows forming geometrical patterns; elements that would be reflected in Hindi films of the 1960s.

Figure 3.2: Inspired by geometrical patterns, which was an important element in the German Expressionism, Shankar (Ashok Kumar) is framed between two geometrically patterned doors in *Mahal*.
Courtesy: Bombay Talkies Ltd.

In the current evaluative tradition as we are used to corporeal monsters and ethereal ghosts, *Mahal* (and *Madhumati*) may not qualify as stock representative of the horror genre, but to look for vicious ghosts in *Mahal* is to judge the film through the standard narratives of the 1980s. Films associated with a genre can change within different contexts. As Mark Jancovich asserts, 'German Expressionist classics like *Nosferatu* (Marnau, 1922) and *The Cabinet of Dr. Caligari* (Wiene, 1920) were rarely seen as horror films in their own day' (2002, p. 2) yet they are now frequently cited as examples of the genre.

As an Indian Gothic, *Mahal* is about Hari Shanker (Ashok Kumar) who buys an old mansion only to find it haunted by Kamini (Madhubala), the ghost of the previous owner's lover. A portrait of the previous owner and their similar looks convince Shanker that he himself is the reincarnation of the former owner of *Mahal*. The legend of the tragic circumstances in which the two lovers had died and Shankar's belief about his reincarnation is reinforced when one day the haunting ghost of Kamini recognizes Shankar as her lover and seeks a reunion. Besotted with the ghost, Shanker plans to kill the caretaker's daughter Asha so that her body can be taken over by Kamini's ghost. But Shankar is whisked away by family and married to Ranjana (Vijayalakshmi) before the murder can be committed.

Yearning for a reunion with his ghost lover, Shankar's belief in reincarnation triumphs over his marital obligations and his wife feeling neglected and abandoned, consumes poison and dies, implicating her husband. Here the plot structure of *Mahal* moves towards a moment of narrative rupture where Freudian identification and estrangement present a causal explanation of an event that was presented as a mystery. With Shankar facing a certain death for the murder of his wife, the daughter of the caretaker, Asha (Madhubala) speaks up. Asha confesses to being the 'ghost' of Kamini. Fed on the immortal love story of the original occupants throughout her childhood, 'a desire to be desired', and identification with Kamini, as she confesses in court, had led her to assume Kamini's identity, wear her clothes, and haunt the *Mahal* in search of true love, wherein she had fallen in love with the photograph of the former occupant, Shankar's lookalike. Why is the previous owner's portrait identical to Shankar? *Mahal*'s secularly inclined narration refuses to engage in the legitimacy of Shankar's belief in reincarnation which is neither approved nor disapproved, even it offers a plausible explanation of the ghost. Asha's masquerade as Kamini's ghost is Freudian identification or the deliberate adoption of another person's behaviour or ideas as one's own: 'a psychological process whereby the subject assimilates an aspect, property or attribute of the other and is transformed, wholly or partially, after the model the other provides' (Laplanche & Pontalis, 1973, p. 205).

Rachel Dwyer's contention that '*Mahal* does not take up great theme of the new nation as did the works of Raj Kapoor and Mehboob Khan' (Dwyer, 2012, p. 130), discounts the self-reflexive ways in which *Mahal* sacrifices its own promising phantasmic narration at the altar of the post-colonial discourse of modernism/rationalism and in a pluralistic spirit of accommodative Nehruvian secularism, discounts one myth to prop up another. It brushes aside the ghost narrative but refuses to engage in the cogency of Shankar's rebirth. The validity of Shankar's reincarnation remains beyond the narration's mandate. The denouement of *Mahal* reveals psychological/temporal illusions at work firmly grounded in a rational world and restores Nehru's modernist, secular world anticipating Dr Anand's (Manoj Kumar) brush with the fantastic in *Woh Kaun Thi?*; Suraj's (Biswajeet) rendezvous with the spirit of a deceased dancer — Kiranmayi (Sharmila Tagore) in *Yeh Raat Phir Na Aayegi* (This Night Won't Come Again); the embalmed body of Rohit (Raza Murad) that goes on murderous rampage in *Cheekh* (The Scream); Dr Rajvansh's (Surendra Kumar) return from the dead in *Do Gaz Zameen Ke Neechay*; the mysterious killer Ajit's (Irfaan Khan) resurrection in *Dhund* (The Fog) (Ramsay, 2003); and Avni's (Vidya Balan) demonic 'possession' in *Bhool Bhulaiyaa* (The Maze) (Priyadarshan, 2007). A detailed exposition of one particular film may help elucidate Hindi horror cinema's negotiation with the imperatives of Nehruvian discourse.

Madhumati

With a Gothic tale of love and redemption couched in Expressionist rhetoric Madhumati's designation as horror is retrospective, and it may be argued that *Madhumati* exhibits only minimal relation to horror. But along with its predecessor *Mahal*, and its successor films such as *Bees*

Saal Baad, Woh Kaun Thi, Kohraa, Poonam Ki Raat (Night of the Full Moon), *Tower House, Bin Baadal Barsaat,* it presents fear both as a subject and effect, and seeks to evoke the feelings of dread not through characters or plots but through crucial genre defining/defying moments. An emphasis on filmic moments instead of contiguous action, as Tom Gunning remarks, allows us to 'highlights the transitions in mode and tone that occur within a short sequence of shots' (Gunning, 2010, p. 7).

For *Madhumati,* I will dwell on two bookended cinematic moments/sequences from the film that mark an abrupt break from the realist conventions that prevail in between *Madhumati's* narration but swivels the plot transiently into the realm of the (ph)antastic marking an incredible rhetorical shift to the Expressionist mode. An overwhelming fantastic quality marks these sequences and set up a cinematic duologue with horror. *Madhumati* opens up on a dark expressionistic night. A car meanders precariously through a rain-drenched road and comes to an uneasy halt as a landslide has closed it. Devendra (Dilip Kumar) and his friend (Nitin Bose) seek refuge in a nearby decrepit *Haveli,* now the refuge of a lone old caretaker. Once inside the mansion a long pan shot heightening suspense appropriates Devendra's view who can fathom an uncanny sense of déjà vu. A dissolve marks the passage of time and later during the night Devendra's sleep is disturbed by acousmatic screams and cries whose source remains unseen. The French critic and composer Michel Chion regards acousmatic sound 'as the unidentified sound that makes us ask: What was that? Where did it come from? Such use of acousmatic sound drives the narrative forward by engaging a character in the film to ask these same questions, and then to seek answers' (Jordan, 2007, p. 125).

An expressionistically spotlighted Devendra makes his way downstairs through a long dark sleepy passage marked by deep shadows. A painting falls off the wall and brings in its wake flashes of memory. A flashback follows.

Devendra recounts his previous birth as Anand, an estate manager for a womanizing Zamindar Ugranarayan (Pran). He recounts falling in love with Madhumati (Vyjanthimala) and being sent away on an errand by Ugranarayan only to find Madhumati missing on his return. Completely dissociated from corporeality yet within a state of ordinary visibility Madhumati's translucent spirit much like Banquo's ghost, manifests itself and exhorts Anand to exact revenge on Ugranarayan. The law enforcer promises help only when evidence materializes. The appearance of *deus ex machina* Madhavi (Vyjanthimala), Madhumati's lookalike, comes to Anand's rescue. Secular ingenuity is brought to bear upon chance arrangement, and Madhavi agrees to impersonate Madhumati's ghost to help entrap Ugranarayan.

As a sequence, the climax in its singularity evokes less of the momentum of the steady genre of romance and returns to the visual conventions of Expressionism. Iconographic patterns seal off this precise moment from the rest of the narration instead making it more archetypal and confessional to the modes of horror. Marking an abrupt break with the realist convention that had proceeded throughout the narration, these visuals script the assemblage of thematic and aesthetic stances that come together again like the introductory sequence, making a covert broad appeal to the genre of horror.

Consider the ghost's entry into the frame which is heralded by thunder and intermittent flashes of lightning, with a howling wind on the soundtrack, curtains flapping like apparition in the breeze casting humanlike shadows on the wall, and nearly threaten to present the viewer with the phantasmic images of a tormented soul. The narration then jettisons abstract symbolism for as much overt embodiment of the spectral as the cinematic techniques of the 1950s could allow. A sudden gust of wind through the window sends the Rocaille chandelier rocking precariously, blowing out the candles perched inside it; and immediately a high camera angle frames a silhouette against a sudden burst of lightening, bringing Madhumati into the frame. As Anand relights the candles, the camera cuts to a low-angled shot to allow the spectators to look right into Ugranarayan's terrified reaction. He recoils in horror and shouts to Anand (Dilip Kumar): 'Ask her to go away'. An unnerved Ugranarayan flinching from the disgusting brush with the undead confesses to his crime and pays for bad Karma. The police officer privy to the confession arrests Ugranarayan. But with Madhavi's arrival afterwards, Anand realizes he has been visited by Madhumati's ghost. Anand follows the mysterious apparition, and falls to his death, much like Madhumati herself, bringing the flashback to a closure. The two lovers united in death are reborn as Devendra and Radha, Anand's wife expected to arrive by train. The narration thus sealed, at the break of dawn Anand drives to the railway station to pick up Radha (Vyjanthimala), the reincarnated Madhumati. This sequence with its aesthetic codes has now acquired a quaint familiarity of the genre, imparting powerful generic qualities to the Hindi horror cinema. With its images, tropes, cinematic vocabulary and a tale of a vengeful spirit that invokes fear, dread and disgust, recall Ugranarayan's flinching away from Madhumati is as much about fear of the dead as the disgust evoked through physical contact with the undead.

Jeanne Hall says that films are best understood in relation to the 'periods in which they were produced and consumed' (Hall, 2001, p. 16). As an archetypical instance of secular-conscious orientations of the Hindi horror genre, *Madhumati* (Roy, 1958) borrows religious constructs specific to Hinduism such as *Karma*,[1] and reincarnation but does not engage in questions of faith or belief. When it does, it subjects the spiritual to the temporal. *Madhumati* (Roy, 1958) signifies what the state-sponsored secular narrative cannot accept or recognize but must deal with by either rejecting or accommodating. *Madhumati* (Roy, 1958) was released a decade after Independence, in an era marked by highly intrusive economic and political actions of an increasingly centralizing state, which included the passage of the Hindu Code Bills that sought to codify, regulate and modernize millennia-old Hindu traditions of marriage, succession, adoption and maintenance. It also introduced provisions for divorce, although marriages in Hinduism are considered sacrosanct and indissoluble. Despite objections from conservative quarters, the social and the political milieu was ready to acquiesce in the subjection of the spiritual to the secular, as embodied in the ghost of Madhumati which can materialize and dematerialize at will, yet desires revenge only through the agency of the state. Anand's words: '*Mujrim apne jurm ki sazaa payega* (The criminal will be punished for his crime)', with the police taking away Ugranarayan takes on extra diegetic resonance. They imply the reaffirmation of the citizen's trust in the workings of the state and its assurance of punishment for the guilty. And with a ghost that 'abides by law', this refusal to wreck vengeance thus allows the state's realm to extend itself not just to the temporal but also to the phantasmal and has two points of significance: first, the phantasmal recognizes the authority of the temporal and its agency the secular state as the sole arbiter, thereby reaffirming faith in its law-dispensing abilities. Second, by submitting itself to secular authority, the spiritual has elevated the temporal over and above itself and thus deified it. *Madhumati* juxtaposes divergent thoughts: in Nehruvian terms it *tolerates* tralatitious traditional beliefs but denies them autonomy beyond that which will bring them in conflict with the modern and the secular. In Freudian terms, that which cannot be recognized but must be dealt with has been rendered harmless and non-threatening. The ideological position of *Madhumati* is more clearly revealed in the climax where, emblematically, the camera captures in a single frame both the ghost of Madhumati with her back to the camera and the police inspector who has come to arrest Ugranarayan, each visible in the other's gaze, positing the coexistence of both the temporal and the phantasmal in a single unifying frame of Nehruvian secularism.

Reconfiguring the relationships between the tralatitious and the modern, through a hierarchy of superior–subordinate relationship, *Madhumati* (Figure 3.3) mythologizes and deifies the secular. Justice reigns supreme, and the secular state stands idealized. Curiously enough, villainy is conflated onto Ugranarayan, the entrenched landed gentry or the Zamindar class that Nehru's India was embattling through constitutional means. The first amendment of the Indian Constitution encroached upon property rights and paved the way for states to frame their own laws abolishing the Zamindari system.

Anand Babu and Madhumati's love affair is foregrounded in the relationship between the tribals and their long-standing land ownership dispute with the zamindar

Figure 3.3: The 'Nehruvian frame' that acknowledges the temporal and the phantasmal in a single frame. Madhumati with her back to the camera along with the police officer.
Courtesy: Bimal Roy Productions.

Ugranarayan. As a class, the zamindars, a creation of the colonial system, were entrusted with tax collection for the colonial regime and could even impose their own tax pauperizing the peasantry. The *Time* magazine succinctly noted the celebration over the abolition of the Zamindari system thus:

> Some 12 million Indians last week celebrated an independence day of their own with laughter and tears, street parades, community songs and free candy for the kids. In the state of Uttar Pradesh it was Deliverance Day, the day that marked the end of zamindari, a system of tax collecting which has held most of India's plain people in thrall since the Middle Ages.... 'The most creditable products of zamindari,' wrote the London Economist, 'have been Rabindranath Tagore, the poet, Liaquat Ali Khan, the Prime Minister, and the Maharaj Kumar of Vizianagram, the cricketer....' The majority have been as vicious as Thackeray's Lord Steyne, as idle as Jane Austen's Mr. Bennett, and as drunken as a Surtees squire. (Time, 1952)

The attempted rape of Madhumati by Ugranarayan is an assertion of the traditional right of a feudal lord: the droit du seigneur or jus primae noctis, the zamindar's right to take his liege's bride on her wedding night. Madhumati's response to this spectacle of murderous consummation and her return from the dead is 'proletarian exigency' on the Zamindari system, aristocratic splendour, and sensuous excesses. Yet Madhumati's vengeance on Ugranarayan through the agency of the state stands as political correctness and ushers in a new age of social change devoid of violence that so often accompanies dynamic social transformation. Ugranarayan's chastisement and Madhumati's vengeance exercised through the apparatus of the state is a reiteration of the justice-dispensing ability of the state and the rejection of vigilante justice. Administering law remains the sole prerogative of the Nehruvian state.

This subgenre of the secular conscious solidified further in the early 1960s when the state appeared strong and invulnerable, and the state's secularization and modernization was seeping into all facets of life on the belief that modernity and scientism could advance only if Indian traditional culturalism could be suppressed, reversed, or even abandoned altogether. With a polity overcommitted to science and reason, the temporal sought not just to tame the spiritual but to dismiss it altogether as 'imaginary', 'chimerical', and 'fantastical'. Whereas the subsequent pseudo-ghost narratives of films such as *Bees Saal Baad* (Nag, 1962), *Woh Kaun Thi?* (Khosla, 1964), *Poonam Ki Raat* (Sahu, 1965) and *Yeh Raat Phir Na Aayegi* (Brij, 1966) are obviously dismissive of the ghost and exemplify their disdain for the phantasmal, the primacy of the empirical over the normative as they unburden themselves of all spectral presences in their denouement, I would like to consider one representative example of the subgenre in which the presence/absence of the spectre is brought to question. *Kohraa* hints at a supernatural presence but its engagement with the ontological presence of the ghost is restricted. Much like Nehruvian secularism where separation of the Church and the state could coexist effortlessly with the intrusive Hindu Code Bill, *Kohraa* maintains a duality in its approach. It hints at a phantasmic presence but like *Madhumati*'s subservience to the exigencies of the secular state and *Mahal's* refusal to broach a final statement on Shankar's rebirth, refuses to grant recognition to the normative.

Kohraa

Kohraa hovers tantalizingly between the exciting hypothesis of the existence of the ghost and a plausible analysis that it does not. The narrative of the fantastic requires unresolved possibilities, and *Kohraa* (Nag, 1964) inspired by Alfred Hitchcock's *Rebecca* (1940) opens with two unresolved mysteries: the mysterious disappearance of Amit Kumar Singh's (Biswajeet) wife Poonam (unknown) and her possible death in a boating accident; and the dubious existence of her ghost. *Kohraa* opens with snapshot-like disjointed sequences: Poonam (always placed strategically off-screen) is getting ready for an amorous rendezvous with one of her many lovers, ignoring Dai Maa's (Lalita Pawar) futile entreaties of amatory restraints. Poonam ventures to her love nest anyway; a shadowy figure appears and fires shots. With one temporal whodunit at hand as yet unresolved subsequently, Raj (Waheeda Rahman) the second wife, finds herself obsessing over another: the 'ghost' of her husband's first wife Poonam (Figure 3.4).

Kohraa's narrative supports the general indeterminacy of fantastic narratives and does not permit us to determine in finality whether the ghost of Poonam haunts the estate or we are confronted with the bitter resentment-induced hallucinations of the hysterical projections of the subconscious fears of a victimized second wife, the *plain Jane* like Raj, who

Figure 3.4: Poonam's spectral presence in *Kohraa* is visible only to Raj and the audience.
Courtesy: Geetanjali Pictures.

dislikes constant comparisons with the previous mistress's more debonair and sophisticated lifestyle and extravagant regime. Caretaker Dai Maa informs Raj of the haunted room of Poonam, and Raj begins to sense a mysterious presence at large that manifests itself during the song sequence, *Jhoom Jhoom Dhalti Raat*, the acousmatic song whose source remains unseen to Raj and which no one other diegetic character seems to hear. The expressionist 'moments' of *Mahal* are recreated in *Kohraa:* the camera anthropomorphizes objects and forces of nature by endowing them with human qualities. Long deserted corridors, shadow glimpsed under doors, mansion with turrets, ornate facades, dramatized frescoes and chairs that move on their own, windows that blow open suddenly are presented in a way as to give them latent physiognomy. Subjective camera shots create abstract art through a juxtaposition of architectural patterns over visuals to create unique geometrical patterns seeking to stage the emotional complexities and agitated states of mind of the principal characters, often framing Raj and Amit Kumar from behind or between architectural constructs. Nevertheless, the supernatural apparition in *Kohraa* appears not to have an objective reality since it remains perceptible to Raj only, and the other bevy of characters do not corroborate Raj's suspicion. The truth for Raj and the audience must remain uncertain and indeterminate. This duality and textual ambiguity resurfaces briefly again in *404: Error Not Found* (Raman, 2011).

How does the narration of *Kohraa* align itself with Nehruvian stance? The haunting, as the film posits, may or may not be real, but unlike *Woh Kaun Thi* or *Bees Saal Baad*, no attempt is ever made to explain these seemingly supernatural occurrences. The narrative engages, but with only temporal affairs. Poonam's mortal remains are discovered from a decrepit car recovered from a dried up lake and Amit Kumar Singh confesses to having shot her dead. At the climax, however, Dai Maa confesses to killing Poonam for her promiscuous life and insatiable infidelities.

With Poonam being dead long before Amit had shot her, Dai Maa's confession seal off an uneasy closure without resolving the presence of Poonam's ghost, and *Kohraa* disturbs phantasmic assumptions to the precise degree that it reinforces it. If the narrative opens with two questions: an unresolved disappearance and the 'truth' about Poonam's ghost, the narrative resolves the former and ignores the latter, laying bare its political propensity. With no murder committed by the husband and no revenge wrought by the ghost, Poonam's spectral presence maintains a mere symbolic presence and its ontological existence remains fundamentally unresolved. The narration subconsciously refuses to intrude into the area of the phantasm/mythic. Conversely, we never find out the (un)reasonableness of the ghost's presence. Precariously oscillating between the possibility of the ghost and the laws of conventional reality, the narration in an accommodating spirit of Nehruvian munificence concerns itself with the temporal, eschews from deliberating on spectral presence, and deals with the temporal affairs. The question of the phantasmic presence of Poonam or her ghost is ultimately rendered irrelevant.

Anti-naturalistic aesthetic via expressionist distortions became a key part of the aesthetic vocabulary of the horror genre in the 1960s, even if few films employed its aesthetic mode to the same degree as *Mahal, Madhumati* or *Kohraa*. Films such as *Bees Saal Baad* (Nag, 1962), *Tower House* (Ansari, 1962), *Woh Kaun Thi?* (Khosla, 1964), *Poonam Ki Raat* (Sahu, 1965), *Yeh Raat Phir Na Aaygi* (Brij, 1966) are substantially if not primarily horror since they oscillate between the laws of conventional reality and the distinct possibilities of the supernatural. Their denouement typifies what I prefer to call as the 'Nehruvian moment' — a cinematic moment that narrows the religious outlook and Indian normative obsession with the supernatural and metaphysical speculation. Past images are recalled again in the denouement to impart them with realist rationalist explications. If these films hold viewers and the diegetic characters in anxious suspense as in *Do Gaz Zameen Ke Neechay* (Ramsay, 1972), *Saboot* (The Evidence) (Ramsay & Ramsay, 1980), *Cheekh* (Bhakri, 1985), *Yeh Raat Phir Na Aayegi* (Sayed, 1992), *Dhund* (Ramsay, 2003), the secular order is reaffirmed through Todorovian uncanny narratives that invite the audience to presume a supernatural presence but conclude by affirming a natural/ secular origin of the 'unexplained'. These films simulate both aesthetically and thematically the narrative structures of the horror genre but offer observable facts and exclude metaphysical speculation. The mise-en-scene of *Bhayanak* (The Terrible) (Syed, 1979) creates the Gothic ambience straight from Hammer production (mis)leading audiences to believe that the members of the family of Thakurs living far off in the woods of the isolated hamlet of Mangalpur are vampires, feeding on human blood. However, the (anti) climax discloses that they merely drain blood from unsuspecting humans through devices that at least superficially look like mammalian horns to offer it in ritualized ceremony to a local deity.

Making considerable profits on small-budget films, the Ramsay Brothers' foray into horror cinema was the most sustained engagement with the genre by any Hindi films production house. With stock plots and staid actors, the Ramsays' inaugurated a new wave in Hindi horror. Working with constrained budgets and inversely proportionate diegetic excesses of blood, gore, sex, and voyeuristic cinematic gaze frequently prying upon bathing starlets, which firmly placed their standardized, assembly-line production films at odds with Hindi cinema's bourgeoisie aspirations, the production house acquired the disrepute of a 'non-metropolitan, non-bourgeois status' (Sen, 2011, p. 198).

Ramsey Brothers' horror films carved out their own niche audience and were quite popular in the 'interiors' — theatres located in working class neighbourhoods of urban areas, semiurban locales and the less sought after 'B' and 'C' exhibition centres. Subtle reasons for their popularity were the elements of sex and sleaze. Since these films were certified with an 'A' (for adults only exhibition), they were out of bound for family audiences and therefore could safely negotiate sexual themes without the fear of losing family audiences. Starting with the walking dead in *Do Gaz Zameen Ke Neechay* (Ramsay, 1972), who turns out to be a living scientist husband Rajvansh (Surendra Kumar) out to wreck vengeance on his unfaithful wife Anjali (Shobhna) and her lover Anand (Imtiaz), when ghosts/monsters did make a comeback in the late 1980s with the Ramsay Brothers' assembly-line production, they became equitable and 'secular' in a Nehruvian sense, being repulsed by and being predisposed to all Indian faiths. *Purani Haveli* (Old Mansion) (Ramsay & Ramsay, 1989) makes extensive use of Christian imagery and bestows 'darshanic' gaze and prophylactic properties on Christian icons. The demonic fiend (Manik Irani) is entrapped inside a church and 'divinely impaled' when a sacred Cross falls from the spire and kills him. The tribute to Nehruvianism is visible in other instances.

In *Nagin* (The Female Serpent) (Kohli, 1976) the lair of the Hindu *sapera* (Premnath) offering amulets to repel an *icchadhari nagin* (form-changing female serpent) sports a frame of Christ on its wall (Figure 3.5).

The ghost in *Kafan* (The Shroud) (Bohra, 1990) can be repulsed in equal measure by an idol of Krishna, an ostentatious display of the Holy Cross and the recitation of the Koran.

Bhool Bhulaiyaa

Bhool Bhulaiyaa's belatedness contributes to its timeliness as it revisits the original vision of *Madhumati*, *Kohraa* and *Poonam Ki Raat* and is a variation of the pseudo-horror

Figure 3.5: The lair of the Hindu priest in *Nagin* sports the photograph of Jesus Christ in top right corner of the frame.
Courtesy: Shankar Films.

films of the 1960s, with the benefit of experience gained in the interim decades and offers explicit psychological resolution. The secular, conscious-oriented narration of the 1960s is remoulded in *Bhool Bhulaiyaa* (Priyadarshan, 2007) where the idea of the phantasmal is posited and reinforced but later dismissed and denied. *Bhool Bhulaiyaa* is secularization of a religious myth and a late post-colonial reiteration of Nehruvian discourse premised on a rationalist approach. The climax marks an elaborate Hindu ritual of exorcism which is but a mere window dressing to carry out a modern psychiatric exercise of catharsis. The Hindu *tantric* ritual allows Avni (Vidya Balan) to live out her fantasy as the 'ghost' of Manjulika, which includes decapitating a dummy of Raja Vibhuti Narayan, her mythical tormentor; the dual personality brought on by the loss of the collective—separation from her grandparent and bound within a shrinking nuclear family. The trauma of 'loss'—her own and Manjulika's is conjoined to produce the compulsion of acquiring Manjulika's personality. In the climax, the empirical asserts itself over the mythic and the 'possessed' Avni is healed, resembling Freud's 'talking cure' for trauma. *Bhool Bhulaiyaa* ends on a defiantly secular/modernist note.

As a dynamic discipline that can permit the staging of different perspectives within its framework without any radical overhaul, the secular conscious narrative may either subject the phantasmal to the temporal as in *Madhumati*; apportion therapeutic values equally among different faiths in repelling evil or even handedly reject all spiritualist claims and conquer evil through secular–non-sectarian means as in *Nagin, Bandh Darwaza, Kafan*; and/or deny and denounce the existence of the phantasmal as in *Mahal, Bees Saal Baad, Kohraa, Woh Kaun Thi, Poonam Ki Raat, Do Gaz Zameen Ke Neechay, Bhayanak, Saboot, Cheekh, Dhund* and *Bhool Bhulaiyaa*. Whereas the secular conscious narratives present different perspectives on faith and phantasm, it subordinates all religious discourses in the public sphere to the expediencies of an overreaching discourse of Nehruvian secular consensus. The early American and the British horror films relied on the narratives characterized by gloom and mystery to put the fear of the unknown at the forefront even as they sought to frighten their audiences through the use of anthropomorphic shadows, creaking doors, empty spaces and eerie atmospherics in films, such as *Rebecca* (Hitchcock, 1940), *The Uninvited* (Allen, 1944), *The Unseen* (Allen, 1945), *The Hound of the Baskervilles* (Fisher, 1959), *Pit and the Pendulum* (Corman, 1961), *The Haunting* (Wise, 1963), *Haunted Palace* (Corman, 1963), *The Innocents* (Clayton, 1961) and *Tomb of Ligeia* (Corman, 1964). This was mirrored by the Hindi horror genre through its initial cycle of horror films that made extensive use of the unseen and evoked fear of the unknown through dark mysterious settings, shadow play, chiaroscuro lighting, surrealistic settings and close-ups that imparted a sense of imminent doom, entrapment and claustrophobia.

Even if *Madhumati, Tower House, Bees Saal Baad, Bin Baadal Barsaat, Kohraa, Woh Kaun Thi? Gumnaam, Poonam Ki Raat* and *Yeh Raat Phir Na Aayegi* were suitably interspersed with elements of romance; their narratives had strong elements of fear and dread. Some of these films surely do possess affinities to other genres, yet undeniably to a significant extent these films also retain the grammar of horror. Films such as *Bin Baadal Barsaat, Woh Kaun Thi?* and *Poonam Ki Raat* were given an 'Adult' certification which differentiates them from the other love stories in circulation about this time. The restricted circulation was meant to exclude certain segments of the audiences — a euphemism for young impressionable minds that may not be able to sieve scientific certainties from normative fiction. This was in consonance with the post-colonial state's belief that a film's significance could shape social subjectivities and could impair or repair its modernization goals. Curiously enough, the same films were suitably 'sanitized' and released on the video format with a U or Universal for All certification. Concurrently, the early years of the genre tended to focus primarily on this Gothic style of the unseen and the dissolution of the human psyche; the later films of the genre began to focus on dissolution of bodies, bodily transformation and deformation. The grotesque and the abominable began to appear in the Hindi horror from around the 1970s through films such as *Do Gaz Zameen Ke Neechay, Jadu Tona, Darwaza, Jaani Dushman*, by which time *The Exorcist* had already set the trend for the same.

Note

1. There is a belief in Hinduism and Buddhism that the effect of a person's actions determines their fate in this life and the reincarnation.

4

Return of Traditional–Cultural Narrative

If the array of secular–conscious narratives in the horror genre was clearly outlined by the early 1970s, the disavowal of the secular preoccupations was also proceeding apace. '[A]s early as 1960s, disagreements arose about the applicability of western notions of secularism (implying the separation of church from state or the idealization of a non-religious political realm) to India' (Gould, 2004, p. 4). As academician T. N. Madan asked: 'The principle question is not whether Indian society will eventually become secularized as [Jawaharlal] Nehru believed it would, but rather whether it is desirable that it should?' (Kaviraj, 1997, p. 343). Despite Gandhi's yearning for a return to the old pristine order devoid of all forms of modernity, including a formal renunciation of modern medicinal practices and the fantastical scheme of reforming unbridled capitalist system through voluntary renouncement and a renewed but reformed commitment to the Hindu caste ideal; the nationalist freedom movement was essentially a modernist discourse not geared to an advancement of the Gandhian ideal. Gandhi's utter distaste for the practices of modern statecraft was matched in proportionate terms, by the bigness of Nehru's dams, which he dubbed 'temples of modern India'. In the early flush of independence, 'the economy was seen to stand for and be capable of resolving any problems that arose in the sphere of culture; technology was in fact the form of politics' (Rajagopal, 2001, p. 32).

However, modernization's promise of a grand redesigning of traditional social relations could not materialize because the Congress' dependence on landowning class made it difficult to push radical land reforms or initiate meaningful land redistribution programmes. Despite the promising abolition of the Zamindari system in the euphoric moments of post-Independence, the Congress became a party with a strong scientific, secular, modernist discourse to peddle, yet wedded to political status quo-ism. By the late 1960s, this Nehruvian modernism which had marginalized the mythic in favour of the scientific/ rational, and the historical/empirical over the normative, floundered in the wake of factors such as Nehru's death, indecisive wars with Pakistan and China, successive droughts, and economic stagnation which was further compounded by the Bangladesh War. The Congress party lost its capacity to engage in any meaningful social change, and instead employed authoritarian means to neutralize the Opposition. This led to the Emergency of 1975. As a fundamental component of post-colonial Indian identity, secularism began to come apart from the mid-1970s in the aftermath of Emergency (1975–1977), which was a critical juncture in Indian polity and produced distinct ideological orientations because the 'Emergency rule undermined the existing structures of popular democracy from which secularism derived its nominal legitimacy' (Upadhyaya, 1992, pp. 828–29).

The discourse of state-sponsored secularism/scientism remained socially confined and was marked by its uneven absorption into the everyday, due to its refraction through multiple resistive cultural and political processes working to thwart its effectuality. Disillusionment with the state system and serious doubts about its justice-dispensing capabilities saw the emergence of the vigilante narratives on the Indian silver screens. The popular response to the excesses of the Congress party was twofold: the rise of political and social conservatism in Indian politics that fructified with the rise of *Hindutva* by the 1990s, and the decline of the Congress and what it apparently professed and embodied: the modernist discourse of scientific rationalism and secularism and modernity. With the development of counter-narratives to the officially sponsored one, the imperative to 'defend' the secular order worth saving in *Madhumati* dissipated and the 'ghost subjugated to the secular order in *Madhumati*, denied altogether in *Bees Saal Baad* (Nag, 1962) and *Woh Kaun Thi?* (Khosla, 1964), made a comeback in the 1970s. As Douglas Kellner notes, 'during eras of socioeconomic crises, when people have difficulty coping with social reality, the occult becomes an efficacious ideological mode that helps explain incomprehensible events with the aid of religious or supernatural mythologies' (Kellner, 1996, p. 218). Enthusiastic reception of a spurt of Hindu mythological films such as *Bhagwan Parshuram* (Lord Parshuram) (Mistry, 1970), *Balak Dhruv* (Dhruv the Child) (Dave, 1974), and the sleeper hit *Jai Santoshi Maa* (Sharma, 1975) cinematically signified general disillusionment with Nehruvian secularism that had marginalized the mythic, and imposed the empirical over the normative. On screen, this engendered the traditional culturalism mode of address in the Hindi horror genre. *Jadu Tona* (Nagaich, 1977) as the prime representative of this subgenre positions traditional, folkloric Hinduism against scientific rationalism and secular ideology. If *Madhumati* subordinates the tralatitious to the secular, *Jadu Tona* fetishizes folklore and presents modernity and tradition as mutually exclusive, thereby initiating a progression that will find fulfilment in *1920* (Bhatt, 2008).

As the predominant mode of address of Hindi horror cinema, the traditional–cultural subgenre requires a more sustained engagement which I shall discuss here. Javeed

Alam describes tradition, as 'transmitted wisdom(s), not reducible to knowledge ... beyond validation or invalidation .... As a past it can be sensed and captured in stories, but unlike history it cannot be told as the story' (Alam, 1999, p. 171). Whereas tradition is affected by religion, it has a much wider definition, manifesting itself through acts of social precepts, ritual praxis, taboos and social engagement. Its area of operations brings it in contact with secular and religious spheres, which can either restrict or amplify its area of operation. Correspondingly, the area occupied by the tralatitious order expands and shrinks as it engages with religious or secular spheres. The traditional–cultural narratives seek advancement of the tralatitious order by undermining the exactitude and certainty of the rational secular order. Cultural appurtenances become sacramental artefacts (*sindoor, mangal sutra,* sacred numerals and calendar art in horror films) are endowed with spiritual values.

Drawing its sustenance from Gandhi's version of an alternative to Nehruvian secular matrix, the traditional–cultural narratives tend to 'counter' secularism and its universalizing tendencies. This tralatitious/mythic/traditional order is aligned not just against the discourse of science and technology and modern medicine but also against the modern secular state apparatus because it marks the dissolution of space between the secular and the temporal. If the secular modernist discourse is increasingly discrete in relation to its constituent parts, the tralatitious/mythic order symbolizes perpetual transmutation in which 'no realm of being, visible or invisible, past or present, is absolutely discontinuous with any other, but all [are] equally accessible and mutually dependent' (Harpham, 2006, p. 51). The aim of the traditional order is to expose the fragility of the modern secular scientific discourse, whereas the consistent and systematic inscription of the mythical order onto the Hindi horror genre narratives points to its pervasiveness.

If the secular–conscious narratives advance and reaffirm Nehruvian consensus and provide a basis for political practices, the tralatitious order advanced by the traditional–cultural subgenre of the Hindi horror cinema is presented as a system of discourse supported by an elaborate system of rituals, sacred texts and insignias. If the modernist discourse has the knout of formal and authoritative law and the secular state apparatus at its disposal, the tralatitious order imposes itself through the sanction of ancient curses and spells that can remain dormant for centuries and generations, yet still wield influence in the modern, secular, scientific world. Despite being subjected to the discourse of medical science, human bodies when possessed by evil spirits in this Hindi horror subgenre respond to and are 'cured' through their acknowledgement of and subjection to the tralatitious order only. Doctors misdiagnose, law enforcers mis-investigate, and modern science offers misexplanation.

The traditional–cultural subgenre is a subalternist resistance to the hegemonic formulations of the Nehruvian era, representing an underworld whose ideas about gender, society and social relations had been largely ignored or overturned in the interest of a modern, secular, postcolonial modern Indian identity. In distinct ways these narratives are moments of dissolution of modernity, about families who despite their modern and secular upbringing live lives at the mercy of terrible, unpredictable malevolent forces beyond empirical comprehension. Its rhetoric seeks to interrogate the certainties established by the secular outlook Hindi horror genre. If secularism, modernity and rationalism stripped the universe of its supernaturalism, conceiving it as an empirically observable reality, the traditional order, espoused by the traditional–cultural narratives are about 'knowing the unknowables' and about the re-inscription of the magical, the mystical and the irrational into the quotidian lived experiences.

The traditional–cultural narratives seek to mythologize the present and the currents of traditional beliefs are kept intact within a modern exterior. The subgenre explores the concept of ancient truth, ignored and abandoned by the modernist discourse of secularism and rationalism, through narratives in which evil entities encroach upon the lives of the principal protagonists, and their struggle with this ancient truth. The normative closure provides the critical framework with which most of the hermeneutically sealed narrative of the subgenre can be read. The denouements mark the overturning of protagonists' previous understanding of their modern world. Though set in a Hindu majoritarian setting and seeking to contemporize Hindu rituals, beliefs and practices, the traditional–cultural subgenre eschews the discourse of Hindu majoritarianism and adopts a reconciliatory, inclusivist tone. Struggle between the empirical and the normative occupies its narrative and affective core.

As a repressed narrative, which has been sealed off in favour of adopting modernity and modernism, the tralatitious order operates subterraneously and surreptitiously within the realm of the secular scientific order and the discursive practices of modern science and technology without being subjected to it. By pointing out failures of the modernist discourse in understanding a system beyond sensory perception, the tralatitious order asserts its superiority over the discourse of science and secularism and exposes its deficiencies in understanding varieties of human experiences. If the secular–conscious-oriented narratives are dismissive of the unknown and the unseen, the traditional–cultural narrative eschew indeterminacy in favour of (sometimes subdued) expressivity employing the conventions of the camera's gaze to force explicit representation on the unknown/unseen and yield meaning that are legible and unambiguous. This realism and temporality bestows phantasmic materiality and space: the 'unseen' becomes the 'seen' demonstrating its perpetual transmutation within the unity of time and space. This difference is evident as the subgenre developed from the 1970s, and prosthetics imparted corporeality to ghosts. The deification of the tra-latitious order necessarily marks the diminutiveness of the modernist discourse.

Like Hindi mythological cinema, it explores discourses that the modernizing imperatives of the secular state have either side-lined or undermined. The diegetic world is more about the means through which annihilation of evil is affected rather than about evil itself. The subgenre asserts that the tralatitious and its cultural pursuits are about constructing a religious identity, to bring back the fence-sitting secularly inclined liberal whose dissenting opinion about, and non-belief in the 'old order' must be revoked and reversed to consecrate his *gharwaapsi* (homecoming). Religion becomes a communicative process, whose potency must be expressed to the non-believing folks and cele-brated. The subgenre attempts the merger of the individ-ual into a larger communal identity. The tralatitious rituals become deified activities whereby the mythic, marginal-ized by the modernist discourse, asserts its potent presence. Importantly, the genre sees the eruption of horror not in the sequestrated geographical neverlands but in the heart of contemporary modern urban landscape.

The narrative of the subgenre valourizes long forgotten and discredited folk traditional practices and through tra-ditionally gendered roles reinforces patriarchy and annihi-lates autonomous female desire. Indic myths are reworked, retold and reinforced, and at the denouement, the secu-lar liberal, who has been admonished and reprimanded through the punishment of demonic possession or ravaged at the hands of an evil entity, finds faith and religion mark-ing his homecoming and return to the realm of faith.

The traditional order, as the sum total of all tralatitious practices deified in films spatially located across decades such as *Jadu Tona* (Nagaich, 1977), *Darwaza* (Ramsay & Ramsay, 1978), *Mangalsutra* (Vijay, 1981), *Gehrayee* (Raje & Desai, 1980), *Chehre Pe Chehra* (Tilak, 1981), *Dahshat*

(Ramsay & Ramsay, 1981), *Veerana* (Ramsay & Ramsay, 1988), *Bees Saal Baad* (Kohli, 1988), *Woh Phir Aayegi* (She Will Return) (Ishaara, 1988), *Junoon* (Bhatt, 1992), *Raat* (The Night) (Varma, 1992), *Suryavanshi* (Kumar, 1992), *Zakhmi Rooh* (Wounded Soul) (Kumar, 1993), *Raaz* (Bhatt, 2002), *Vaastu Shastra* (Varma, 2004), *Krishna Cottage* (Varma, 2004), *Eight: The Power of Shani* (Razdan, 2006), *Gauri* (Akbar, 2007), *Phoonk* (Varma, 2008), *Raaz 2* (Suri, 2009), *13B* (Kumar, 2009), *Mallika* (Louis, 2009), *Rokk* (Stop) (Ransinghe, 2010), *Ragini MMS* (Kripalani, 2011), *Ghost* (Bedi, 2012), *Horror Story* (Raina, 2013) and *Ragini MMS 2* (Patel, 2014) are a celebration of the varieties and diversities of folklores and cultural practices that the secular order has disavowed and disowned. The practices of this amorphous tralatitious order presented through 'narratives of faith', has no grand theory to offer but offers resistance to the totalizing effects of state-sponsored discourse of secularism/scientism through insignificant tralatitious acts.

The traditional discourse is fetishized and resistance is offered through tralatitious events that erupt onto the narratives of the subgenre. Coercive cinematic techniques like the close-up that impart intensified spectatorial implications for the audiences and cutaway shots along with zoom in that divert attention and focus on isolated elements within the frame imparts potencies to specific elements of the mise-en-scène, endow them with heightened presence and penalizing authority, and the ghost materializes in all its glorious latex prosthetics and crude display of animal innards. What explains the change in the emphasis on the 'aesthetics of subtleties' of the horror flicks of the 1960s, such as *Kohraa, Bees Saal Baad, Woh Kaun Thi?, Poonam Ki Raat*, to the 'aesthetics of prosthetics' of Nagaich, the Ramsays or the Bhakri Brothers? What marked the advent of the bluntness of the Ramsays productions in the 1970s and what accounted for its decline in the 90s? Sangita Gopal's contention that the horror was completely absent from the screen till the 1970s and the few films before that dealt with the supernatural were 'old fashioned ghost stories ... less concerned with the horrific than with the extra empirical dimension of the human' (Gopal, 2011, p. 93) overlooks interesting aspects of generic formulations.

Content is (re)formatted when genres meet new audiences, and the codes and conventions of horror change over time. Aesthetic sensibilities come not from any inherited or inner aesthetic sense but from an individual's location in a densely stratified social system—aesthetics is a strategy of class distinction signifying social distance and differences, and taste itself is defined to quote Pierre Bourdieu in terms of the 'distaste of the taste of others'. The aesthetic sensibilities exhibited by different groups are defined in terms of opposition to one another. The horror films of the 1960s exhibit a bourgeoisified 'sense of distinction' that in Bourdieuian sense warrants the primacy of 'form over function, manner over matter and celebrates the pure pleasure of the mind over the coarse pleasures of the senses' (Wacquant, 2008, p. 271). The aesthetic strategy of the Ramsays was an inversion; of function over form, of (over)representation over the understated, of the triumph of the taste of necessity over the sense of distinction. While both the horror films of the 1960s and the 1980s seem to converge in their thematic concerns, were they addressed to the same spectatorship? The answer to this necessitates a distinction between spectatorship and audience. While the 'audience is an empirical category referring to the actual individuals who frequent the cinema, the spectator is a theoretical concept that stands for the viewing position arising from the text's strategies of representation' (Prasad, 2000, pp. 161-62). Through their strategies of the aesthetics of excess, the Ramsays had constructed their ideal reader–spectator.

The fantastic worlds of *Mahal, Madhumati and Kohraa* were deeply indebted to German Expressionism whose aesthetic strategies intended to 'make the cinema respectable for bourgeois audiences and give it status of art' (Elsaeser, 1989, p. 32). But Indian urban space witnessed remarkable demographic changes from the late 1960s onwards and suggested an interesting shift in cinema's aesthetic sensibilities. The rise of the Ramsays from 1970s onwards and their brand of brash, direct cinema coincided with changing demographics across Indian metropolises. Indian cities witnessed a large influx of young migrants from campestral, agrestic spaces into slummy metropolitan expanse. Surreptitiously patronized by the local political class as vote banks this assemblage would flock to the cinema on a regular basis and emerged as a boisterous but committed patron of the Hindi cinema. In the 1970s, the trope for the Indian cinema as Ashish Nandy puts it turns out to be 'the slum's point of view' (Nandy, 1998, p. 2). This cinema of the 1970s that saw the foray of the Ramsays into the horror genre, stressed on directness, vigour, crudity and lower middle-class sensibilities, 'catering to a restless, transient population hustling for goods and attracted to a cinema of sensation and distraction' (Vasudevan, 2003). Horror was not the only genre that catered to this restless spectatorship seeking the cinema of thrills and sensations. Linda Williams groups together horror, pornography and melodrama as genres that signify systems of excess (Williams, 1991). The absence of a separate Indian porn industry meant horror genre with its adult certification became the perfect surreptitious transferral for the soft porn industry that emerged in the exhibition circuits from the early 1980s. Concurrently, statutory regulations that required cinema halls to offer a set number of tickets at discounted rates for the 'front benches' and price control further distorted audience demographics, and the consequent proletarianization of the cinema audiences engendered changes in themes of cinema in conformity with new demographics. By the 1980s, the middle class had retreated from cinema halls for the home comforts of the VCRs and the TV sets, 'leaving cinema halls for the "children of the mean streets"' (Athique, 2011, p. 152). But I am overreaching here. Let us examine the ways in which the tralatitious order asserts itself cinematically.

Jadu Tona

The traditional order exerts pressure on the statist discourse and provides resistance through Bakhtinian *carnivalesque* moments. Non-obeisance to the *peepul* tree, spilling
of vermillion must necessarily portend the coming of evil;
and the wailing of a cat, the focus on the icon framed on
the wall are moments heralding the arrival of the exiled.
The traditional–cultural narrative of the Hindi horror films
are marked by elaborate punitory systems where the most
innocuous violation of the smallest act of omission of the
most innocent tralatitious tradition must invariably become
an act of sacrilege and blasphemy requiring discipline and
punishment, wherein belief is rewarded and unbelief is
punished. *Jadu Tona* (Nagaich, 1967) marked the inaugural
moment of the subgenre. Released at much around the same
time when narratives of revenge dramas and vigilantism
were undermining the authority of the secular state, *Jadu
Tona* undermines the State's empirical/scientific narrative
as it presents religion not as a system of ideology geared
to political advancement but as a way of life. Expectedly,
the release of the film coincided with the resurgence of conservative political parties such as the *Jan Sangh*, with the
Janata Party espousing economic and cultural conservatism.
In the traditional–cultural mode of representation of Hindi
horror genre, the cinematic tropes of the Hindi horror are
Hindu dominated but not necessarily Hindutva oriented. If
Jadu Tona is about 'the return of the traditional', it becomes
crucial to understand what meaning of tradition is being
invoked, articulated and expressed, for it is through these
sequences that traditional beliefs are at once 'experienced',
sanctified and awarded dignity. The uncanny emerges in
response to the subject's crisis in dealing with modernity.
Cultural inclusivity marks the scopic regime of *Jadu Tona*.
Seeking to establish the primacy of faith over reason, the
voiceover in the opening sequence seeks to establish beyond

any reasonable doubt the existence of unclean spirits with the sceptical audiences by quoting 'scriptural evidence' in the Hindu *Puranas*, the Koran and the Bible, accompanied with an inter-title: 'For those who believe in God, and universally accepted creation: Known or Unknown' (Figure 4.1).

Positioning itself at the intersection of modernity and tradition, *Jadu Tona* is about Ameer Chand (Prem Chopra) whose teen daughter Harsha (Baby Pinky) is possessed by a 'wronged' spirit, which then goes on a murdering spree to punish its tormentors. While the unsuspecting father seeks out a more secular scientific treatment through psychiatry, the police officer Jolly Goodman (Ashok Kumar) much like Lieutenant F. Kinderman (Lee J. Cobb) in *The Exorcist* (Friedkin, 1973) suspect the girl's involvement in

Figure 4.1: The admonitory still that defines the orientation of the narrative from *Jadu Tona*.
Courtesy: Guru Enterprising Movies.

the mysterious murders. The evil spirit is expelled and the daughter is eventually 'recovered' by the tantric who had earlier been contemptuously rebuked by the family.

Chand's opprobrious refusal to pay *pranaam* (obeisance) to a peepul (Bo) tree at his ancestral villages' entrance sets the tone for eventual possession. His daughters the younger Harsha and the older Varsha (Reena Roy) deride Hinduism's folk tradition and refuse to apply *kala tikka*, or a spot of kohl on their forehead, to ward off evil eye, as they go out sightseeing. Interestingly, the concept of the evil eye has a supra-communal appeal, and finds resonance in the Islamic belief system as *buri nazar* (evil eye), with well-known and widely circulated instances of the Prophet being affected by black magic and at least one Koranic verse speaking of women who blow on knots and cast spells.[1] Thus, the family's refusal to 'honour' tralatitious Hindu folk tradition excludes them from the protection that folk tradition offers, anticipating *Junoon* (Bhatt, 1992), where Vikram's (Rahul Roy) hunting expedition on a full moon night despite requests to the contrary from villagers sees him transformed into an accursed feline as a punishment for disbelieving in the local myths. With the context thus established possession emerges as a 'punishment' for flouting traditional norms. The girl child Harsha wanders off to a ruin and is possessed. Interestingly enough, the villagers are not only aware of the haunting in the ruins, they are assured; well-nigh certain Harsha has been possessed by the spirit of Panna Lal. The constitutive parts of the village's cultural ecosystem is accommodative enough to admit the phantasmic 'Other'; the living and the undead coexist, each maintaining and honouring the realm of the other. The ghost does not venture out of the ruins. The living do not venture near the ruins. Varsha's violation of this tradition invites punishment. Exorcism called by the grandparents is stymied by Varsha, whose secular scientific modern values and disbelief in demonic possessions leads her to send Baba Bajrangi (Premnath), the *tantric*, packing. The family returns to Bombay and a modern, secular discourse is introduced through the psychiatrist cum amateur pilot Dr Kailash (Feroz Khan), who dismisses the possession hypothesis and instead diagnoses Harsha's changed voice and superhuman strength during 'fits' as symptomatic of split personality disorder. The inclusivity and heterogeneity of this traditional narrative is introduced through the acknowledgement of another faith's therapeutic 'offer'. Harsha has a fit during a joyride in Dr Kailash's biplane bearing number '786', nearly bringing it down. But Dr Kailash survives and Jolly Goodman as a witness breaks the 'fourth wall' thereby extending himself beyond the fictional world to address the audience directly: 'If it wasn't for that number, Dr Kailash, this might have been your end' (Figure 4.2).

Figure 4.2: Police Inspector Jolly Goodman breaks the fourth wall and points out the significance of the Islamic numeral 786 in *Jadu Tona*.
Courtesy: Guru Enterprising Movies.

In one instance the emotional involvement in the story is interrupted with a moment of critical detachment, thereby creating a mix of identification and awareness. The figure of 786 has profound religious significance in South Asian Islam and is considered equivalent to the Koranic text, *b-ismi-llāhi r-raḥmāni r-raḥīm*, meaning 'In the name of God, the Most Gracious, and Most Merciful', *Jadu Tona*'s narration reflects the inclusionary traditional culturalism of the 1970s, as it skilfully acknowledges the potency of Islam in neutralizing evil. The ghost is exorcised and Harsha is 'cured' by the village tantric through a ritual of Hindu exorcism witnessed among others by Varsha and Dr Kailash.

In the denouement, a subjective overhead shot of Chand bowing down to the blessed Bo tree at his village's entrance marks his final reconciliation with the traditional. The evil spirit departs but not before it has 'performed' elaborate ideological tasks: exacted revenge through its own agency, thereby 'recovering' the liberty surrendered to the temporal in *Madhumati*; discredited the scientific rationalism championed by Dr Kailash and won new 'converts' in Varsha and Ameer Chand who realize the potency of the tralatitious. *Jadu Tona*'s vigilante resolution undermines the State's authority, deified in *Madhumati*, and scripts the return of the repressed or in Lacanian terms, an eruption of the real into the symbolic. Yet its breach does not overwhelm the secular citadel. Instead it works out a compromise in its resolution where each claimant offers its own explanation for the 'possession' and none is dispossessed of legitimacy. Dr Kailash still gets to offer a positivist explanation of the 'cure'. Harsha, he points out in the climax, was a copybook case of split personality and had been cured through a well-documented psychical treatment known in medical parlance as 'crude psychic treatment'. The discourse of law and its course of action are all but discounted from the narrative of *Jadu Tona*; the murders that take place are never adjudicated upon by law, poetic justice reigns supreme, the secular state stands undermined, and Harsha is exonerated of all moral responsibility. The film also positions an ethnographic correlation that would authentically become a convention of the horror genre: the literates ignore and dismiss what the preliterates/oral traditionalists honour and exalt.

Gehrayee

The secular public sphere under strain in *Jadu Tona* further shrinks in *Gehrayee* (Raje & Desai, 1980), which reiterates this split between the contemporary and the primeval and like *Jadu Tona* offers another reproachful and admonitory inter-title early on: 'For those who believe, no explanation is necessary — for those who don't, no explanation is possible (Figure 4.3)'!

If *Jadu Tona* is about deification of folk practices, *Gehrayee* presents an exclusionary modernity couched in Cartesianism and successfully seeks to replace 'faith in demonstration

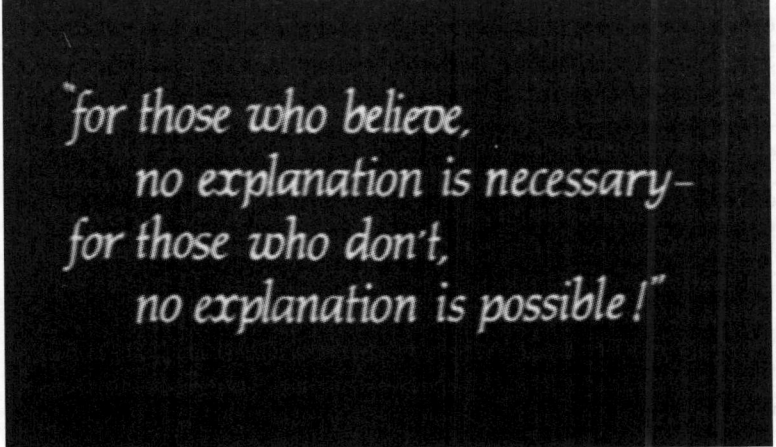

Figure 4.3: The rebuking inter-title that defines the traditional–cultural orientation of *Gehrayee*.
Courtesy: Avikam.

and verification' by 'faith in belief'. Everything not in consonant with this generalizability of Cartesianism stands
demoded and excluded by Chennabasappa (Shriram Lagoo)
who refuses to believe that his daughter Uma (Padmini
Kolhapure) is possessed until proved otherwise through
the crude Hindu exorcism offered in the climax. By abjuring
any prosthetic innovation in Uma's transformation when
she is possessed, *Gehrayee* uses the aesthetics of realism and
naturalism to affect a heightened and a more pronounced
cinematic denunciation of the empirical discourse of modernism. Uma's possession is effectuated through change of
her demeanour, from demureness to the outright slattern.
Development and industrialization is the central premise
and as a post-Emergency horror film *Gehrayee* is about a
middle-class entrepreneur Chennabasappa whose unrelenting faith in reason, rationality, and 'exclusionary modernity'
stands reversed in the denouement. As an anti-modernist
discourse the narrative of *Gehrayee* builds up the climax
through a series of proleptic moments, each premonitory
instant unfolding as a bad omen that in its conclusiveness
culminates in Uma's possession leading the family to first
engage with the discourse of science to 'cure' their daughter
and then revert to the application of the unscientific.

Gehrayee's central narrative premise is between two
worldviews in conflict. Modernity and traditionalism are
refigured in Chennabasappa, the bearer of Nehruvian
conscience who has lately sold off his ancestral estate for
buying into bourgeoisie aspirations of self-owned home,
and who desires that his daughter Uma's sickness (Padmini
Kolhapure) be treated as per medical and proven scientific
treatment. The rebellious son Nandu (Anant Nag) intends
to invoke a more traditional non-scientific treatment, cinematically mirroring the generational conflict of the post-
Emergency politics. The audience cued by the preceding
ominous clues empathizes with Nandu, whose attempts to
invoke traditional exorcism are impeded by Chennabasappa.

Chennabasappa's disdain for the tralatitious and the pre-modern verging on contempt is presented in *Gehrayee*'s ambiguous, deft and economical opening sequence. When inspecting his estate Chennabasappa suddenly chances upon a snake and wants to kill it, but is restrained by Baswa, (unknown) the caretaker, who believes the snake is a guardian of the family and the estate. *Gehrayee* thus represents a yearning for the re-establishment of the harmonious relationship between man and nature.

Baswa's plans for the upcoming sowing season on the estate stand thwarted by Chennabasappa's plan to abandon his property, abdicate his responsibility over an inconvenient inheritance: the burdensome guardianship of his estate which he eventually sells to a soap manufactory. 'Others will be inspired similarly and slowly the whole area will develop' is how he reasons. Baswa is given marching orders and promised rehabilitation which never materializes. Baswa's passive eviction from his land by the absentee landlord shapes his anger into apoplectic rage, and the narrative trajectory adopts an allegorical position of events occurring off-screen. Baswa's anger is the anger of the dispossessed, legitimized against Chennabasappa's obdurate intentions to impose a modernism discourse on the unwilling.

Chennabasappa emerges as secular, his modernism discernible in his exhortations to Nandu to go on the field trip regardless of the *amavasya*, and his mocking advice to his family at the dinner table not to perform any rituals on his own death. Thereafter a series of unfortunate incidents follow. Chennabasappa's son Nandu (Anant Nag) ventures on *amavasya* (moonless night) and meets with an accident. Uma's academic grades fall (Padmini Kolhapure), and at home her mother encounters another profanation: vermillion on Uma's soles. Under spells of possession, Uma becomes a sexual predator seeking to seduce her own brother, even as she imperils her parents' marriage by revealing Chennabasappa's sexual escapade with his caretaker Baswa's wife.

As in *Jadu Tona*, demonic possession in *Gehrayee* is an act of vengeance, wrecked by the caretaker Baswa who worshipped the estate as mother and for whom selling off land to the manufactory is akin to rape. While the identification of geographical entity with Mother Earth recalls the conflation of the anthropomorphic maps and initial configurations of Indian nationalism that often imagined the nation as a Divine Feminine, the caretaker's dislocation draws attention to the estimated 25 million people displaced involuntarily by development projects in the first 50 years of the post-Independence years (Robinson, 2003, p. 2). Blatant and wanton exploitation of natural resources directly impinged upon the livelihood and subsistence of the marginalized culminating in the *Chipko* movement that had erupted on the national stage a few years before the film's release.

Chennabasappa belongs to the English-educated class of entrepreneurs, bureaucrats and civil servants that came to identify most closely with Nehru's secular and development-oriented outlook and concurrently gained the most from state-planned economic development. Chennabasappa's modernism is an unrelenting march towards bourgeoisie respectability, evident in his utilitarian approach, and observable in his insensate decision to introduce labour-saving machineries in his own manufactory, even when it leads to layoffs. It is akin to the development projects of the preceding decades that led to displacement of millions. As a moral dilemma, possession exposes Chennabasappa's limitations as a caring father, whose paternalism has been shaped by his cold and unflinching faith in the reasons of science, and his ready acquiescence in the debilitating shock treatment offered by a psychiatrist even though it does not ameliorate Uma's condition.

This suppression of the primeval by the unrelenting Chennabasappa finally disintegrates as the repressed order surfaces and Chennabasappa redefines his relationship with the unknown, albeit now from a position of subordination. Baswa, as a protagonist, has transformed from an obedient flunky to a vengeance seeker—his revenge appears as the revenge of the internally displaced against forced migration, large-scale development project and against insentient utilitarianism. Paradoxically, despite efforts to the contrary, the Nehruvian State's development discourse in many ways recreated the excesses of the colonial state that it sought to replace. The Indian political elite looked upon poverty as an appendage of modernity that had already arrived; economic disparity merely demanded management of poverty through relocations of slums not their elimination. In the name of productivity and efficiency, the modernist state sought disengagement between economics and politics, engendering social imbalance, destruction of life support systems, and reckless exploitation. Cartesian–Hume ontology provided the ideological justificatory ground to this liberalism.

Like Dickens' Ebenezer Scrooge in *The Christmas Carol,* whose stinginess and moral turpitude though despicable by moral standards is highly efficient since it bears the spirit of the Protestant work ethics, Chennabasappa's introduction of capital-intensive technology in his workplace despite moral apprehension of layoffs is morally reprehensible but consonant with the modernizing state's twin goals of economic efficiency and convenience. Baswa's exploitation, degradation, and finally expulsion from Chennabasappa's estate is reprehensible but only in a moral sphere. It is this rupture between politics and economics that provides the fig leaf to Chennabasappa's immoral acts: because they are 'convenience and efficient'. Baswa's expulsion and the seduction of his wife by Chennabasappa are absolved because if the former is productive, the latter was convenient, much like Chennabasappa's reasoning with his wife Saroja (Indrani Mukherjee): 'It was just companionship for an afternoon'.

Despite the socialist rhetoric, the Nehruvian State had morphed and mutated into an inefficient capitalist entity running a monopoly over resources, and seeking its justification on highly dubious moralistic grounds of public welfare. *Gehrayee* represents not just the moral horrors of corporate capitalism but of disengaged rationality, which created ground for a rupture between economics and politics. This disjuncture could allow a non-moralist, modernist post-colonial state to take various contradictory postures on various positions of life and offer different justificatory reasons for each. Thus, displacement stood morally vindicated on grounds of larger social good even if it meant destruction of the relatively few. Nevertheless, *Gehrayee* does not only present a critique of modernity, rather it implicitly picks and chooses the forms of Hinduism it deems fit to pit against Chennabasappa's modernity. Towards the denouement, an exorcism mocked and refuted as mumbo-jumbo by Chennabasappa stands vindicated. Chennabasappa wins back his daughter but his faith in modernity and its efficacy lies in tatters. Like Chennabasappa's venture capitalism in *Gehrayee*, the desecration of an old abandoned Christian graveyard to make way for a five-star hotel in *Hotel* (Ramsay & Ramsay, 1981) and the dumping of pollutants into a lake used by Hindu worshippers in *Raaz 2: The Mystery Continues* (Suri, 2009) in the name of mercantile values bring about supernatural retribution in their wake. *Raaz 2* is placed firmly within the matrix of the traditional–cultural matrix as Yash (Adhyayan Suman), the journalist who makes his dough out of debunking Hindu myths and tantric practices in contemporary Indian society in his top drawing reality TV show *Andhvishwas* (Superstitions) must not only confront the hence repressed discourse but must also pay for his unbelief. And in *Bhoot* (Varma, 2003), computer engineer Vishal (Ajay Devgn), who has chosen to live in a high-rise duplex despite the real estate broker warning that the previous occupant had jumped to her death, must affirm his belief in the 'unseen' when his wife Swati (Urmila Matondkar) is possessed by the spirit of its previous occupant.

Phoonk

Similarly, *Phoonk* (Whiff) is about a temple whose consecration at a construction site is being held up by the liberal Rajeev's (Sudeep) unbelief in either God or Evil. His construction workers discover a rock which bears a quaint resemblance to Lord Ganesh and want to put a temple dedicated to the deity. But Rajiv turns their request and warns his staff that 'he can't change his foundation plans for these superstitions'. At different narrative junctions, Rajeev's dissenting and transgressive (dis)belief is the only obstruction to the temple's materialization. Even his wife Aarti's (Amruta Kanvilkar) pleas for the temple are dismissed, and Rajeev becomes the only impediment whose intransigence deters the emergence of a consensus on the temple, on which everybody else seems to agree.

Soon Rajeev discovers that his trusted business colleagues have cheated him and dismisses them after ritual humiliation. Later a mid-close-up shot captures an angry Rajeev contemplating the embezzlement with his wife in the background where he deplores this 'breach' of faith by his trusted aides; even as an idol of Ganesh is lighted up sporadically in the foreground, implicitly calling his own lack of faith in question. Rajeev bemoans the transgression of faith of his colleagues and indulgently celebrates another (Figure 4.4).

The decontextualized fetishization of an idol of Ganesha at home and a calendar art featuring Hanuman accommodates the narrative's fascination with the traditional orientation. The eventual possession of his teen daughter Raksha (Ahsaas Channa) is as much a product of Rajeev's disbelief as a reaction to it. His embezzling business partners know Rajeev lacks faith in either divinity or malefic forces or demonic possession and resort to black magic, secure in the belief that Rajeev's rejection of faith will prevent him from

Figure 4.4: The Ganesh idol with Rajeev and Aarti in the background in *Phoonk*. *Courtesy:* Ace Movie Company.

taking recourse to necessary spiritual countermeasures. Rajeev reacts in ways his business associates want him to.

If the numeral 786 had introduced the subtext of an all-inclusive spirituality in *Jadu Tona*, Raksha experiences a fit of possession in which the sound of a temple's chiming of bells and *Azaan* are heard simultaneously implying that evil is pitted against all faiths, not necessarily Hinduism alone. Corresponding to the preliterate grandparents in *Jadu Tona* and the house servant in *Gehrayee* who 'believes' in possession, *Phoonk* has Rajeev's mother who 'believes' in black magic, but Dr Seema Walke (Lilette Dubey) diagnoses the child with dissociative personality disorder, blaming the grandmother's fantastical bedtime Hindu mythological stories as the trigger for her split personality. As Raksha is admitted to a hospital, Rajeev finally reconciles with faith and allows the temple to come up at the site of its discovery, marking his admission into the tralatitious order. The climax intercuts with the labourers performing puja at the construction site with visuals of Madhu (Ashwini Kalsekar) performing black magic. Rajeev disrupts the rituals and Madhu is killed. The liberal atheist who had been 'holding out' gives way; secular dissent is silenced, and Rajiv returns to the fold of faith. Paradoxically, *Phoonk*'s narrative closure marks a symbolic exchange of worldviews between

Aarti and Rajeev. While Rajeev has witnessed the exorcism and is now a believer and a 'convert', Aarti has lost her faith and credits Dr Seema Walke's treatment as the cure. *Phoonk*'s denouement marks the eternal struggle between the normative and empirical *Weltanschauungen* but also shows Aarti bearing 'false consciousness'. She believes Raksha's cure is through modern medicine, not faith. As a modernist Rajiv was assertive and domineering and non-accommodating; as a convert to the traditional order he becomes non-threatening and accommodative, refusing to contradict Aarti. Nonetheless, non-believing Nehruvian liberal Rajiv eschews his neutrality and converts to the creed of the spiritual.

The Horror in Science Fiction: Between Morals and Mad Scientists

If the ghost/*pret atma*-driven narrative is about marking off the human from the divine, the corporeal monster-driven plots of the Hindi horror genre are about threatened human integrity, and the horror-inflected Hindi science fiction genre with its dominant paradigm of the reconstitution of the human body essentially remains another manifestation of the traditional–cultural genre — an anti-science discourse. These monster narratives as 'moral tales of scientific excesses' dramatize the troubled place of science in the post-colonial Indian condition. I take up the science fiction genre to the extent that it features monstrosities that evoke fear and dread.

Horror and science fiction together can be defined as narratives of the 'fantastic', not just 'because the boundaries between them is extremely permeable' but also because they 'tell stories of impossible experiences that defy rational logic and currently known empirical laws', (Sobchack, 1996, p. 313). Sobchack notes that science fiction developed out of the traditional horror film, which was sufficiently technologized to suit the aesthetic demands of a post-industrial audience. Drawing a distinction between horror and science fiction genre is difficult, 'and often articles and books on science fiction and horror discuss the same or similar films' (Cook & Bernink, 1999, p. 191). Manfred Nagl suggests that 'fantasy, horror and SF [science fiction] films inextricably overlap … and in the case of SF films, it seems more helpful and less sensible to start not from the concept of sharply divided, mutually exclusive typologies but from that continuous scale with broad transitional zones or a field essentially constituted by three poles — horror, fantasy, and SF' (Nagl, 1983, p. 263). Others have sought to differentiate between the genres in terms of their aesthetics and the affective response they generate in spectatorship. 'The major visual impulse of all SF films is to pictorialize the unfamiliar, the non-existent, the strange, and the totally alien' (Sobchack, 2001, p. 88). On the other hand, Noel Carroll includes science fiction within the horror genre when SF 'substitutes futuristic technologies for supernatural forces' (Carroll, 1990, p. 14). For Susan Hayward, the monstrous in the horror film 'is visited upon us for us to deal with', in science fiction genre, 'we deal with our monstrous potential' (Hayward, 2006, p. 207). Dawley's *Frankenstein* (1910) forged an alliance between the two genres of horror and science fiction and later films such as James Whale's *Frankenstein* (1931), *The Bride of Frankenstein* (1935) and *Island of Lost Souls* (Kenton, 1932) are distinct instances of hybridity between horror and science fiction. This alliance was redefined later in the apocalyptic catastrophe/mutant narratives of the 1950s, featuring monsters that were the creation of a 'science gone wrong'.

My purpose here is to reconnoitre the monster/creature narrative or the horror-inflected science fiction of Hindi cinema, contextualize and explore the historically specific monstrous visions in the two pioneering narratives of *Chehre Pe Chehra* (Tilak, 1981) and *Dahshat* (Ramsay & Ramsay, 1981) and investigate the monstrosities created by or through science which 'most typify what is considered by some to be miscegenation of the two genres' (Sobchack, 2001, p. 30).

Historicity of the Monstrous Narrative

The discourse of the monster narrative in Hollywood manifesting through films, such as *The Day the Earth Stood Still* (Wise, 1951), *The Beast from 20,000 Fathoms* (Lourie, 1953), *War of the Worlds* (Haskins, 1953), *Them!* (Douglas, 1954), *Tarantula* (Arnold, 1955), *Invasion of the Body Snatchers* (Siegel, 1956), *The Incredible Shrinking Man* (Arnold, 1957), *The Amazing Colossal Man* (Gordon, 1957), *The Fly* (Neumann, 1958) and *The Beast of Yucca Flats* (Francis, 1961) articulated cultural and social anxieties of their age, and 'critical acceptance of this genre emerged from the ashes of World War II' (Katovich & Kinkade, 1993, p. 621). The late 1950s, which marked an upsurge in the genre, roughly corresponds to the dawning of the nuclear age, growing American anxieties about the atom bomb, the Soviet's Sputnik endeavour, paranoia of an impending nuclear holocaust, the 'hunt for the Reds', and to the Cold War. As Mark Jankovich claims, 'most critics of the decade's invasion narratives [saw] them as being intricately linked to Cold War ideology' (Geraghty, 2009, p. 119). Science fiction cinema flourished particularly well in Eastern Europe during the Cold War, perhaps because of the opportunities the genre offered for 'covert social comment' (Kuhn & Westwell, 2012, p. 360).

While the monster-inflected Hindi horror cinema emerged only amid the din of the anti-science discourse of the 1980s, the historicity of the Hindi science fiction can be traced to Kishore Kumar starrer films such as *Mr. X in Bombay* (Soni, 1964), and *Shreeman Funtoosh* (Mr. Funtoosh) (Soni, 1965), which were more in the genre of 'comic science fiction fantasies' rather than any serious discourse on science, and they marked Bombay cinema's preliminary brush with the genre. On a serious note, *Chand Par Chadayee* (Trip to Moon) (Sundaram, 1967), a B-grade Indian science fiction released in the aftermath of South Asian crises such as the Chinese nuclear test of 1964 and the inconclusive Indo-Pak war of 1965 was a serious attempt at the genre and like the cautionary Klaatu (Michael Rennie)-led *The Day the Earth Stood Still* (Wise, 1951) gave vent to Indian rhetoric on global nuclear disarmament and the magniloquence of the non-alignment movement. It narrates the tale of an Indian astronaut Captain Anand (Dara Singh) who is kidnapped by a benign alien race and taken to *Chandra Lok* (Moon) to face trial as a stand-in for mankind's transgressions 'with hydrogen and atom bombs'. The rhetoric of the Non-aligned Movement (NAM) is hard to miss in the intergalactic jury's accusatory tone, when Anand's offer of interplanetary collaboration is contemptuously dismissed as: 'cooperation from those who interfere in the internal matters of others ... those who can't live with their fellow brothers and neighbours.' However, these were mostly B-budget productions, driven more by the lead star's persona or comic digressions than by the science fiction plot itself.

Despite a Bakhtinian *dialogism* where Bombay cinema has often awaited genres and pyrotechnics from Hollywood, Hindi cinema largely remained aloof from the monstrous narratives. The scientific and technological feats such as the Indian nuclear test or the launch of the indigenous space programme from the mid-1970s onwards did not spark off any invasion from space/mutation/mutant genre in Hindi horror cinema because arch rival Pakistan's modest scientific endeavour did not produce national anxieties in India, the way Soviet Union's *Sputnik*-led scientific enterprise did for the American public opinion. The prospects of Pakistani Patton tanks rolling down the Indian plains of the Punjab appeared far more threatening than Pakistan's scrimpy scientific ingenuity. Monsters that ran amok in the 1970s

Hindi horror cinema such as Thakur Sahib (Sanjeev Kumar) who periodically metamorphoses into a wolf man in *Jaani Dushman* (Kohli, 1979), or Nagin (Reena Roy) the shape-changing female serpent in *Nagin* (Kohli, 1976) were derivatives of traditional Hindu folk beliefs, not science. Bombay cinema did not produce any 'science fashioned monster' right until *Chehre Pe Chehra* (Tilak, 1981) and *Dahshat* (Ramsay & Ramsay, 1981). Hindi science fiction genre itself has seen success mostly limited to the superhero genre films such as *Mr. India* (Kapur, 1987), *Koi Mil Gaya* (Roshan, 2003), *Krrish* (Roshan, 2006), *Ra.One* (Sinha, 2011), and *Krrish 3* (Roshan, 2013).

What distinguishes *Chehre Pe Chehra* (Tilak, 1981) and subsequently *Dahshat* (Ramsay & Ramsay, 1981) from other Hindi horror films is, first, the presence of the corporeal monster whose manifestation is rationalized in the context of scientific causality. As an interstitial being the monster is caught between two worlds but belongs to neither. The *pret atma* (evil soul) can subvert the physical laws of space–time and causality, the monster cannot. Second, the manifestation of the monster in these narratives articulates anxieties about science's troubled place in the post-Emergency Indian milieu. With moralistic overtones, *Chehra Pe Chehra* (henceforth CPC) and *Dahshat* share not just narrative complicities but also mark the conflation of science and horror by 'playing off' these apprehensions.

It becomes pertinent to contextualize and explore the historicity of the monster narratives of the Hindi cinema. Even if the specificity of the monstrous narratives can be located within the anti-science discourse of the 1980s, one must understand that unlike in the West, the Indian Renaissance which came 300 years later was about returning to the Vedas not abandoning it. With its caste-driven social hierarchy, rigid compartmentalization of social interaction, and its obscurantist — sometimes insensate practices — Hinduism seemed far more threatened by social sciences than natural sciences. The Indian Reformation pioneered by the social reformers of the eighteenth century was consequently geared to advance ideas of social equality not Newtonian gravity. Most of these Hindu reformist movements did not mark a distance from the scriptures, rather a return to it. 'Neither Swami Dayanand, nor Swami Vivekananda nor the Brahmo *Samajis* are remembered for emphasizing the scientific traditions of India's past' (Gupta, 2010).

With no dogmatic view on genesis, creation or the evolution, Hinduism did not require any rethinking of its core concepts, and in the absence of a sacred book and fixed doctrines, 'it had *ipso facto* to be tolerant of all views as there was nothing that could be considered as heretical to the nucleus of its faith' (Alam, 1999, p. 178). Science could challenge Hindu practices not the Hindu cosmic view of life, and even when the Indian scientists of the late nineteenth and early twentieth centuries aspired to secular nationalism and rationality they 'repeatedly sought to situate their science in relation to a distant explicitly "Hindu" past' (Arnold, 1999, p. 156). The methods, activities and principles which are typical to science made minor inroads into Indian mysticism and 'scientific temper never had a chance to loosen up the Hindu cosmopolis' (Nanda, 1999, p. 1068).[2]

Even if the post-colonial state was ready to acquiesce in the subjection of the spiritual/mythical to the secular/ temporal by the late 1970s, disillusionment with the secular/ modernist discourse in the post-Emergency period saw the return of the repressed traditional order in the horror genre through plotlines that fetishized Hindu folklores. As explicit denunciations of science, *Chehre Pe Chehra* (Tilak, 1981) and *Dahshat* (Ramsay & Ramsay, 1981) signify the countercurrents against scientism and secularism of the 1980s even as they endeavour to acquaint us with monstrosities begotten by science and cinematically dramatize science's troubled post-colonial position. The monster-like the ghost becomes a public agent for renewing faith in the mythic order and appears as 'a creature of religion' (Ingebretsen, 1998, p. 91).

India and the Discourse of Science

Nationalist sentiments could, as need be, in opportunist ways, appropriate or disown science. The nationalist leaders during the freedom struggle phase condemned the West for precisely those virtues in which the West took pride: modernization and industrialization. Yet post-Independence India saw the aesthetization of the 'cult of technology' in the public sphere by Nehruvian economics, for whom dams were but 'the temples of modern India'. Nevertheless, post-Independence endeavours at inculcating scientific temper had to contend with 'the religious-cultural traditionalists, [who] assisted by revivalistic tendencies ... kept up an anti-science movement and remained alienated from the efforts towards a national science policy' (Sharma, 1976, p. 1961). The 1958 resolution adopted by the Indian Parliament, which identified the goals of the Indian science policy as being to encourage, 'individual initiative for the acquisition and dissemination of new knowledge' (Sharma, 1976, p. 1969) did not succeed in ushering any scientific cultural revolution.

The Indian elite proposed, 'technological rather than political and moral solutions to the problems of poverty, inequality and environmental damage' (Mishra, 2005). With economic planning, science moved into the realm of administration and management, and the Indian bureaucracy pursuing the aims of the Indian bourgeoisie presented internal displacement, retrenchment from work as inherent and inevitable on the long march to the Western mode of development and economic prosperity. Large-scale industrialization through forceful land appropriation merely served the well-entrenched pre-capitalist economic forces further implicating science in oppressive Indian social structures.

By the late 1960s, the empirical/modern narrative floundered and the excesses of the Emergency shattered trust in public institutions. The optimism of the early decades was overshadowed by the late realization of consequences of science-driven development projects whose affects were being felt in the 1970s most notably with the *Chipko* Movement. The devastating effects of the development projects under centralized planning were thus apportioned to science, signifying a general disillusionment with the Congress party and its avowal of scientific secularism. The 1970s marked the return of the mythological narratives in Hindi cinema, which had been hitherto banished from public discourse. In the 1980s, science came under attack and paradoxically united an assortment of right- and left-wing opinions against itself. Driven by an anti-modernist discourse these anti-science sermons sought the deification of a supposedly more environmentally friendly Indian (Hindu) past. For the India's Left, science like any ideological state apparatus, had emerged out of capitalist institutions, geared to advance venture capitalism, and had been introduced during the colonial era by an insensate colonial regime. Its Eurocentricity and complicity in Western imperialism coupled with its later *avatar* as an explicit instrument of transnational corporations rendered it suspect in Third World development projects.

The Hindu nationalist ideology and environmental issues developed in tandem from the late 1970s and 'certain environmental movements consciously or unconsciously expressed themselves in ways that aid[ed] articulation of revivalist and nationalist Hindutva thought' (Sharma, 2011, p. 6). For the Hindu Right, science disputed the normative, traditional knowledge of the Indian masses. This convergence of opinions against science led to a counter-science movement in the 1980s wherein attempts to bring scientific rationality to bear upon traditional, cultural and normative practices evoked hostile responses. The supposedly all-encompassing meta-narratives of Western science were to be countered by the micro-narratives rooted in indigenous cultural terms. Science was to be celebrated but only if it reaffirmed ancient wisdom and attested to the 'common sense' of Indian culture. Universalizing tendencies of scientific temper was seen as no better than the traumatic totalizing imperial experience, where Western ontology had reduced the diversities of colonized societies and of human experiences itself to mere statistics and subsumed the marginal into the subliminal, 'flattening out' both the sacred and the profane, paralleling the two practitioners of science, Dr Wilson (Sanjeev Kumar) in *Chehre Pe Chehra* (Tilak, 1981) and Dr Vishal (Om Shivpuri) in *Dahshat* (Ramsay & Ramsay, 1981) who embark upon the conquest of human nature and challenge the corporeal integrity of the human body by seeking to reconstitute it into simple binary terms of good/bad and efficient/inefficient. *CPC* and *Dahshat* share several fundamental premises and cinematically aestheticize a late post-colonial response to the science in question.

Monstrosities from Science or Monstrous Science?

A series of transgressions against nature and anxieties about science distinguish the narrative of *Chehre Pe Chehra* and *Dahshat* from other Hindi horror films. As exuberant fantasies of biological transformation the two monster narratives imagine a new moral order and historical–civilizational change aided and abetted by scientific discipline. Despite their alleged altruistic aims, doctors/scientists in these narratives invariably create creatures outside the natural order of evolution. Far from being presented as mad, these narratives present scientists as 'rational' and 'calculating', fully aware of the moral dilemma that their work involves, including the mortal risk that their scientific endeavour poses to others. Both the narratives present science and its practitioners as dogmatic, distant, self-centred, and wholly divorced from moral economy, paralleling the Nehruvian development projects of the preceding decades. The discourse on science in *CPC* and *Dahshat* couched in the traumatic colonial experience and contemporary Indian practices figuratively re-enact and allegorize certain historical events familiar to Indian filmgoers.

As an Indian adaptation of R.L. Stevenson's *Dr. Jekyll and Mr. Hyde*, *CPC* was the inaugural moment for a science begotten lusus naturae, presenting Hindi moviegoers with a pure distilled monstrosity instead of the usual *pret atma* (evil soul)-driven plot. *CPC* opens with a public conference at a town hall wherein Dr Wilson presents his claims of being able to effectuate a physical separation between 'evil impulses' and 'good intentions' inherent in the seemingly indivisible human nature, making humans 'perpetually good'. He thereby envisions the internalization of the Panopticon, wherein the human body would be perpetually placed under an eternal moralistic gaze from within, and made permanently disposed to moral excellence. Dr Wilson's grand scientific vision to impose a 'regime of discipline' on the human body recalls Foucault's assertion that 'societal transformation of every epoch is associated with the manipulation, control and disciplining of the [human] body' (Foucault, 1973). If Foucauldian bipower is 'an explosion of numerous and diverse techniques for achieving the subjugation of bodies and the control of population' (Foucault, 1998, p. 140), Dr Wilson's bipower is designed to make the human body socially compliant and morally efficient. And it is precisely in this 'imposition of goodness' from within that betrays totalitarianism in Dr Wilson's science, and marks a Foucauldian disciplining of the body.

The crowning moment of Dr Wilson's (un)ethical experiment conducted on himself, manifests later when he metamorphoses into a simian like subhuman monstrous entity marking the successful separation of the *Id* and the *Superego*. Holding Dr Wilson's point of view, the camera rotates 360 degree rapidly destabilizing the fixed position of the viewer and images of his fiancée and his friend David appear and disappear from Dr Wilson's reverse angle position in successive dissolves. Initiating a brief non-diegetic reflection, the camera slows down to focus on a now transformed Dr Wilson who peers into a mirror, breaks the fourth wall and addresses the viewer directly: *Now call your God and show this to Him* (Figure 4.5)!

How does Dr Wilson's science position itself against the traditional order? Looking into the mirror is a common trope in classical cinema connoting vanity and a surplus of the Self. And Biblical passages such as 'Let us make man in

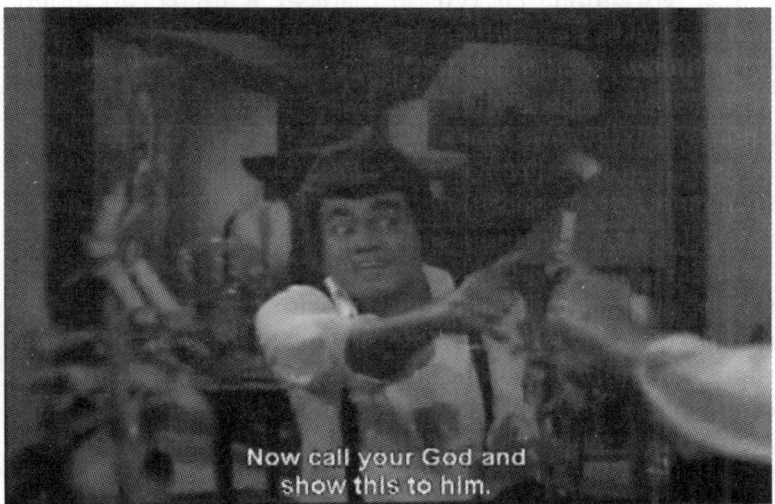

Figure 4.5: Dr Wilson's (Sanjeev Kumar) moment of self-aggrandizement in *Chehre Pe Chehra*.
Courtesy: Tilak Movies Pvt. Ltd.

our image, and after our likeness' (Genesis 1: 26–27); 'In the likeness of God made he him' (Genesis 5: 1); 'In the image of God made He man' (Genesis 9: 6); 'Man … is the image of and glory of God' (I Corinthians 11: 7); and 'Men which are made after the similitude of God' (James 3: 9) under-line the fact that Christian faith considers the human body as being made in the image of God. Dr Wilson's scientific achievement comports two connotations: the separation of the *Id* from the *Superego* is an act of Creation duplicated suc-cessfully in a laboratory, open to observation and replica-bility in the two scales of science. Second, the experiment scripts a successful desacralization/secularization of the human body away from a divinely engineered *Genesis* and characterizes its submission to a secular scientific modern-ist discourse. Through his science, Dr Wilson redefines and refigures the human body, and thus it is here that his sci-ence becomes an act of profanation and blasphemy and a challenge to the traditional/mythic order.

If a workaholic Dr Wilson (Sanjeev Kumar) can indefi-nitely postpone his gratification and his marriage to his betrothed Diana (Sulakshana Pandit) by sublimating his sexual energy into scientific creativity, his periodic transmutations into Mr Black (Sanjeev Kumar) symbolically distances Dr Wilson from his own acts and unleashes his untamed *Id* which driven by primitive instincts spends its energies in raping Daisy (Rekha). Despite sufficient know-ledge of Mr Black's exploits, Dr Wilson continues to believe that his scientific invention and knowledge is an oppor-tunity to be exploited. His compensation to Daisy for the rapes committed upon her by his *Id,* with vague assurances of protection precognitively parallels the much-vaunted Nehruvian development projects of the earlier decades that displaced millions and forced large-scale migration on the marginalized. As a foreshadowing of the Bhopal Gas tragedy, *Chehra Pe Chehra* is all too prescient. In the denoue-ment, Dr Wilson remorsefully affects reconciliation with faith. He dies at the altar of the very church whose spiritual proficiency he had earlier denied and denounced, as he seeks expiation of his guilt ridden (con)science through a confession. This marks his return to faith, a symbolic *ghar waapsi* or homecoming.

The Horror of Transmutation

In *Dahshat* (Ramsay & Ramsay, 1981), Dr Vishal aims to conflate several evolutionary qualities within the human body and anticipates the ethical dilemma of cloning that forms the central premise of *Jaane Hoga Kya* (What Will Happen?) (Barretto & Mohla, 2006), where scientist Siddharth's (Aftab Shivdasani) defiance of his institutional head Dr Krishnan's (Paresh Rawal) counsel 'not to mess with God's creation' creates a malefic, murderous clone who eventually runs riot.

Dahshat is equally subversive of the paternalistic science fathered in the heydays of Nehruvian secularism. The sexagenarian Dr Vishal (Om Shivpuri), emblematically representing the Nehruvian generation, believes man's body to be imperfect and experiments with animal serum and stolen human body parts in the hope a creating a race of superhumans endowed with animal strengths, even as the theft of corpses from the local cemetery fuels speculation that the dead are rising. If Dr Wilson desires the creation of morally efficient human being for whom being immoral/evil will never be a conscious choice, Dr Vishal seeks to endow the human body with evolutionary discipline, that of imparting the human body with multiple evolutionary qualities: the ocular proficiency of hawks, the olfactorial sense of canids. As he confesses to a younger Dr Sameer (Naveen Nischol): 'Human body is incomplete. It does not possess the capabilities that animals do'. Dr Wilson's explicit vanity in *CPC* is matched by Dr Vishal's secrecy and discreetness in running a clandestine science project and conducting immoral experiments on unsuspecting patients. His disavowal of all responsibility for his patient's death from an unprincipled experiment is again a reaffirmation of disinterested scientific attitude and science's troubled place in the modernist context. Dr Wilson's mutation into a monstrous seething beast marks his regression into an animal, beyond self-control, both metaphorical and otherwise. If Dr Wilson eventually reunites with faith, Dr Vishal dies remorseless and unrepentant, shot dead by the police.

As spatial layouts devoid of all material comforts Drs Wilson's and Vishal's dimly lit and cramped laboratories indicate how their architectural design ignoring human comforts has subordinated its occupants to the exigencies of an exacting science. The architectural 'discipline' becomes an extension of the discipline that penitentiary institutions impose upon the human body. These two cautionary tales suggest that there must be something inherently authoritarian in the essence of science. When these science practitioners regress back to subhuman conditions, they undermine the long-held sacrosanct traditional concept of the integrity of the human body, and when they transmogrify into quintessentially grotesque spectacles then the scientific order can no longer be defended. Thus, the narratives of films like *CPC* and *Dahshat*, while marking the capacity of science and technology to overrule corporeality, offers us the construction of 'new industrial bodies' and articulate the moral and cultural anxieties of the 1980s. These narratives deify a conservative perspective in which the traditional order appears as the much better alternative.

The Triumph of the Traditional/Mythic Order

By the 1990s, the practitioners of science were either made redundant or rendered safe and assimilable to the creed of the 'Mythic Order'. A counter-narrative to this alleged

Western science did not mean rejection of science per se, but merely rearticulating modern scientific rationality in terms of indigenous traditions.

In *Veerana* (Ramsay & Ramsay, 1988), the psychiatrist brought in for Jasmine's fits soon realizes that she is possessed and is killed while fleeing from her. In *Shaitani Ilaaka* (Ramsay, 1990), Dr Yograj called in for Anjali's (Sri Prada) incurable nightmares inspects her room, declares it to be haunted by an evil spirit and refers her to a tantric baba (Surinder Pal) in Tibet. In *Raat* (Varma, 1992), Dr Chari (Anant Nag) 'misdiagnoses' demonic possession as a case of schizophrenia. The prefatory sequence of *Raaz* (Bhatt, 2002) opens with Professor Agni Swarup's (Ashutosh Rana) diatribe against modern medicine practices even as doctors are administering medical treatment to a possessed woman: 'You cannot treat this disease because you can treat humans' only not wayward spirits. But you will not believe me, since it does not suit your profession'. In *Aatma* (The Soul) (Ramsay, 2006), disbelieving Dr Aman Mehra's (Kapil Jhaveri) wife Neha (Neha) is possessed, culminating in the couple's 'return to faith' in the denouement.

In *Shaapit: The Cursed* (Bhatt, 2010), Professor Pashupati (Rahul Dev) imparts the legitimacy of a scientific discourse onto the occult as he runs a 'Society for Paranormal Studies' (Figure 4.6).

In *Help* (Virani, 2010), Aditya Motwani (Shreyas Talpade), the exorcist, is an academician and a 'board certified psychiatrist' who has documented cases that offer 'hard evidence that the phenomenon [of demonic possession] is real'. In *Ragini MMS 2* (Patel, 2014), Dr Meera Dutta (Divya Dutta), a trained American psychiatrist who specializes in paranormal cases, is not only a believer in the possession thesis but an exorcist herself. Even the cybernetic shape-shifting monster Ra.One (Arjun Rampal) in the science fiction *Ra.One* (Sinha, 2011) shares deep cultural kinship with Hindu mythology and exploits the religiosity of the Hindu

Figure 4.6: Professor Pashupati's society where he imparts the legitimacy of an academic discourse on the Occult in *Shaapit: The Cursed*.
Courtesy: ASA Productions and Enterprises.

epic Ramayana. The evil Ra.One's ability to regenerate itself through auto-construction parallels Ravana, the mythical demon king of the Hindu epic *Ramayana*. These 'disabling of science' scenes can be read as marking the assertions of the repressed mythical/traditional order.

Interestingly, films like *13B* (Kumar, 2009), *3G* (Anand & Chibber, 2013) undermine instrumental rationality of electrical appurtenances and the ghostly presence surfaces not from tombs, or haunted mansions but from electronic devices (Figure 4.7).

The flat 13B in a high rise is a refuge for restive souls who can undermine the operational self-sufficiency of electrical devices and incidentally turns them into the 'medium' of contact from the world of beyond. The narrative imposes the phantasmal over the technological and denies all functional autonomy of Newtonian physics and Ohm's law; ghosts broadcast mysterious messages on TV sets, cell phones do not work within the precincts of their realm, light bulbs explode, and a prescient television serial *Sab Khairiyat Hai* (Everything's Alright) runs exclusively for Manohar's (Madhavan) family alone presenting the household with entertainment culled from the family itself. In the *Horror Story* (Raina, 2013), the maleficent soul of the criminally

Figure 4.7: Manohar (Madhavan) confronts the operational autonomy of electrical devices in *13B*.
Courtesy: Reliance Big Pictures.

insane Maya (Sheetal Singh) resides of all places in an electronic machine.

Through these narratives, non-modern subjectivity finds its cinematic expression. If science and technology depersonalized and dissociated the individual from his social surrounding by objectifying social relations and shattering the individual's sense of primordial identity, these narratives recuperate and enable the subject to adapt to a technologized, depersonalized, secular urban landscape, providing a timeless continuum from the constant change inherent in modern experience. I now move on to another subgeneric mutation of the traditional–cultural narrative—monstrous 'Other' feminine narratives—aligned against the secular/modernist discourse of modernity over issues of female subjectivity and sexual differences.

The Monstrous 'Other' Feminine

Reversing the normative traditional mode of the female-in-crisis scene in the horror genre, *Veerana* (Ramsay & Ramsay, 1988) opens with 'masculinity in crisis' setting. A would-be male victim pleads for mercy, to which Baba (Rajesh Vivek) mockingly retorts, 'Nikita will slake her thirst with your warm blood today'. A silhouette appears as the casting rolls off and a pan shot brings Nikita in focus, holding a phallic-looking dagger and dressed in an ultra-feminine, black, lacy gown that partially compensates for her masculinization. With her controlling gaze fixed on the male victim, signifying her superiority in the psychological relationship of power, she soon turns into a hideous monstrosity and carries out a ritual disembowelment of her victim. A disembodied voice introduces Nikita as a *naapak jism*— an 'abject' body—the site of sexual perversities and moral transgressions. Men ensnared into illicit sexual encounters with the centuries-old witch in her more alluring form, which belies the evil within, are waylaid and killed. Her recourse to a behavioural trait that is considered typical of men and her male victims' emasculation, represented by the phallic dagger with which she 'penetrates' them, mark their symbolic castration. Nikita, the seductress is doubly abject. Positioned on the cusp between the living and the dead she routinely transforms herself into a beautiful woman from her true, disgusting, abject, non-human self. Second, she also operates outside the ambit of sanctified social relations and lures men with offers of illicit sex and uninhibitedly transgresses the boundaries of female propriety. Female desire 'offloaded' on to an interstitial, immor(t)al, female body thus stands doubly 'abjected'. A more extended discussion of *Veerana* is reserved for a later section, but here, in Barbara Creed's terms, Nikita is the prototypical representation of female monstrosity. If woman is the image and man the bearer of the look (Mulvey, 1989), in a clear reversal of roles, Nikita, the monstrous female is the beholder of the scopophilic gaze and objectifies the male. Her gaze becoming the erotic basis for her pleasure, sexual or otherwise.

Coming in the wake of the second feminist wave and having imbibed Freudian psychoanalysis, semiotics, structuralism and Althusserian Marxism, Laura Mulvey (1989), Barbara Creed (1993; 2002) and Linda Williams (2002) deconstructed the gaze[3] and the popular representation of women in cinema, which had an impact beyond Western film theory. While the monstrous feminine of Hollywood (Creed, 2002) is available transhistorically over much of cinema across the world, the female monster of Hindi horror cinema remains ignored and merits serious academic exploration. The preoccupation with male monsters led Western film theorists, mostly men, to discuss 'female monstrosity either as part of male monstrosity, or as man's castrated other … including insinuations that "there are no great female monsters as in the tradition of Frankenstein's monster or Dracula"' (Creed, 1993, p. 3).

Carol J. Clover (1992), Barbara Creed (1993; 2002) and Linda Williams (2002) have extensively elaborated on art horror's brush with gendered monstrosity. For Julia Kristeva, the 'abject' which 'does not respect borders, positions, rules: the in-between, the ambiguous, the composite' (Kristeva, 1982, p. 4) must be excluded, expelled and kept in abeyance and placed on the imaginary other side so that the living object continues to exist because it threatens to take us back to that primordial moment of birth. The most primitive of these 'in-betweens' is the moment of birth, when we were both inside and outside the mother, alive yet not born, in a state that defies taxonomical description. It is this moment of 'immemorial violence that lies at the base of our beings' (Hogle, 2002, p. 7) threatening us with chaos and from which we must forever separate ourselves. The base of our existence, always calls us back, and yet we distance ourselves from this abject moment in order to define ourselves as a subject.

Kristeva locates the source of horror in the pre-oedipal stage, in a child's attempts to break away and become a separate subject. The abject confronts us from within in 'our earliest attempt to release the hold of the maternal entity' (Kristeva, 1982, p. 13). Abjection is a necessary precondition of narcissism, allowing the child to take its proper place in relation to the symbolic order 'of language, law, morality, religion and all social existence' (Baldick, 2008, p. 327). It is in the child's attempt to free itself from the mother and her refusal to let go that the mother becomes abject. In her psychoanalytic study *The Monstrous Feminine*, published in 1993, Creed asserts that horror cinematic texts serve to illustrate the Kristevan 'abject' in three ways: first, by presenting us an array of bodily waste and putrefying flesh; second, the ghost/monster metaphor as an interstitial 'other' defies taxonomy and challenges boundaries between the human and the non-human; and third, through the monstrous maternal figure, 'the abyss, the monstrous vagina, the origin of all life threatening to reabsorb what it once birthed' (Creed, 2015, p. 56) such as the archaic mother figure in films such as *Psycho* (Hitchcock, 1960), *Carrie* (dePalma, 1976), *The brood* (Cronenberg, 1979) and *Aliens* (Cameroon, 1986).

Much of the monstrous imagery constructed in Hollywood horror genre with regard to the female monster — here I refer to Barbara Creed's monstrous feminine — 'is built in conjunction with her reproductive and mothering functions' (Creed, 1993, p. 7). While I agree with Creed's views that horror texts indeed serve to illustrate abjection, the monstrous feminine needs to be understood outside this framework of the mother–child relations; because unlike the classic oedipal situation, the son as numerous Hindi films explicate, 'rises to avenge the loss of [his mother's] status as a *suhagin* (the bride), and doesn't seek to replace the father' (Gabriel, 2002, p. 118).

The monstrous feminine as an archaic mother figure finds no resonance in Hindi horror cinema. Instead I posit that a subgenre engendered in the 1980s, which I term the monstrous 'other' feminine narrative, as an offshoot within the Hindi horror cinema's traditional–cultural narrative presents an interstitial phantasmal female monster, with wanton sexual desires and gaze, as the abject 'Other'. What differentiates this subgenre from other horror films?

Through narrative closures, traditional gendered perspectives are reinforced, normative femininity is deified, and the monstrous other feminine, commanding sovereign female desire and controlling gaze is annihilated. Through the monstrous other feminine narrative the tralatitious order elides the modernist discourse of gendered sexual equality and instead reaffirms male sovereignty over female desire.

Exorcism becomes the means not only of expelling the interstitial phantasmal being but also for punishing and disciplining the female body for uninhibited desire and gaze. If Creed's monstrous feminine is about the archaic mother refusing to let go of her child, the monstrous other feminine of Hindi horror cinema refuses to let go of desire and gaze. I focus on films that depict females as villainous ghosts that threaten the extant moral and sanctified sexual order and hope to show how these Hindi horror narratives of the interstitial female monstrosities, with their subtext of repressed sexuality and projection of fear and longing belong to the traditional/cultural trappings, even as they prime themselves for Freudian analysis.

This section will consider the role that gender plays in the articulation of monstrosity in Hindi horror cinema and trace the inaugural moment of the 'monstrous other female' as a subgenre within Hindi horror cinema, mapping narratives in which female sexuality *is* the monstrosity. Pertinent is the question: In what ways has the monstrous other feminine subgenre narrative met the collective need of patriarchy? Whereas Freud speaks of female genitals as being frightening to the male, I hazard the generalization that the fear is couched in the male's perception of the alleged 'surplus' sexuality that seems to reside in the female body. This abundance of desire, beyond reproductive needs, is delegitimized both socially and conventionally in this subgenre of the Hindi horror film and presented as a clear threat to the instituted phallocentric order.

The discursive strategies of 'monstrous other feminine' narrative marks new aesthetics, carefully regulated access to gaze that fetishizes and disavows the female form, and a mise-en-scene that enacts male fantasies, asserting deep-seated anxieties about granting sexual autonomy to the female that can be traced back to the 'Colonial Encounter' of the nineteenth century. The imagination of the nation-state in the nineteenth century as a 'corporeal being' coupled with the deification of motherhood and cartographical representation of the nascent nation state as *Bharat Maa* or Mother India, did not look upon the maternal figure as either monstrous or malefic. Rather the period saw 'an alternate tradition … in which the nation [was] cartographically presented to its subject-citizens … as mother, woman, goddess' (Ramaswamy, 2001, p. 97). Even the Hindu ideal feminine construct of Sati–Savitri–Sita, the mythical triad of devotional wives committed to chastity and fidelity, was 'wholly a product of the development of a dominant middle class culture coeval with the era of nationalism' (Chatterjee, 1989, p. 248). Cloaked in Hindu mythology that legitimized Indian tradition, women of the hearth were exalted and glorified amid apprehensions that females in the public sphere would generate disruptive identities.[4] Deification of Hindu women as non-sexual figures of maternity became necessary to facilitate their entry into the outside world.

The post-colonial Nehruvian State sought a reversal of these entrenched forms of patriarchies. The Hindu Code Bill of the 1950s empowered Hindu females by awarding them equal property rights. Concurrently, the introduction of colour facilitated film producers to cash in the picturesque foreign locales and Bombay cinema introduced a diegetic bourgeois spatial–temporal space where romance could be conducted uninterrupted, away from the disciplining patriarchal gaze, and songs came to acquire an unmistakable erotic appeal. Conventional demureness of the 1960s was replaced by the Westernized open sexuality by the 1970s. Burgeoning population led the State to direct its gaze in regulating sexual relations. Concurrently, family planning which was a state subject until 1976 was made a concurrent subject with the 42nd amendment passed during the Emergency, paving the way for the federal government to promote birth control measures. State-sponsored family planning programmes and initiatives inadvertently pitted women's reproductive rights against normative patriarchal practices. The dissolution of the traditional joint-family system furthered female empowerment by removing assertive patriarchs, and 'the 1980s saw the emergence of the vocal and visible autonomous women's groups which placed feminist issues firmly on the public agenda' (Menon, 2004, p. 169).

Films such as *Sanjog* (Coincidence) (Balan, 1971), *Julie* (Sethumadhavan, 1975), *Insaaf ka Tarazu* (Scales of Justice) (Chopra, 1980), Jeevandhara (Life Stream) (Rao, 1982) and *Mujhe Insaaf Chahiye* (I Want Justice) (Rao, 1983) heroically narrativized the feminine struggle against middle-class conventionalities, oftentimes undermining patriarchy and most often allowing a valourized but deviant female sexuality to escape unscathed with the audience's sympathy. The masculinization of the lead female figures collapsed the traditional categories of gender, and the notions of transgressive sexuality that they professed without causing public outcry was a further dissolution of patriarchal values. The 'mannish' woman suggested a new sexual independence and threat to male sexual identity. The monstrous other feminine emerged as a counter-narrative to this feminist discourse.

If the 1970s Hollywood slasher genre presented sexually active females being punished for sexual transgression by the monster/killer, the Hindi horror genre of the 1980s engineered the 'monstrous other feminine', a sadist, neurotic and narcissistic *pret atma* (evil soul), as the monstrosity who as the possessor of gaze and desire, threatens sanctified familial relations by seeking to imbricate herself within heterosexual monogamous relations and invites (divine) punishment for defying the symbolic order. The monstrous other feminine was a patriarchal riposte to this assertive feminist discourse, emerging as a subgenre from within Hindi horror cinema in much the same way as the 'bitches from hell'[5] narrative of the 1980s was Hollywood's backlash against 1970s' feminism, which, as Susan Faludi notes, 'shaped much of Hollywood's portrayal of woman in the eighties ... [wherein] the "good mother" wins and the independent woman gets punished' (Faludi, 1992, p. 141). Unlike Hollywood's monstrous feminine, this subgenre of Hindi horror cinema sought to displace abjectness and monstrosity, not on to motherhood, but on to the cultural and social 'other' of motherhood: 'the monstrous Other feminine' who stands outside socially sanctioned conjugal relations, marking a neat demarcation of the mother and the demimondaine. With its competing sets of female sexualities, this monstrous other feminine subgenre of Hindi horror cinema plays out Freud's return of the repressed 'other'. As the threatening 'Other' that seeks to subvert phallocentricity through the appropriation of desire and gaze, the monstrous other feminine is vanquished in the narrative's closure and the status quo of normative femininity is preserved.

The inaugural moment in the female-centred horror/ monster film cycle is invariably *Madhumati* (Roy, 1958), in which the ghost of Madhumati (Vyjanthimala) returns not only to seek vengeance on her molester Ugranarayan (Pran) but also to kill her lover Anand Babu (Dilip Kumar) so as to unite with him through reincarnation. Again in *Nagin* (Kohli, 1976), the shape-changing serpent Nagin (Reena Roy) is seeking revenge on a group of friends responsible for her ophidian mate's death. But I situate the monstrous other feminine as a distinct entity from other female ghosts. *Madhumati* and *Nagin* are sympathetic characters, their monstrous urge driven purely by the desire to avenge the disruption of conjugal domesticity. Beneath their guileless monstrosity, they are very much traditional, moral Hindu women. The 'monstrous other feminine', desirous of another woman's man, is a home wrecker, a fallen woman and a disruptor of domestic conjugality. *Mangalsutra* will be analysed hopefully in ways in which it can distinctly delineate the more general tendencies of similar thematically organized films such as *Bees Saal Baad* (Kohli, 1988), *Veerana* (Ramsay & Ramsay, 1988), *Woh Phir Aayegi* (Ishaara, 1988), *Suryavanshi* (Kumar, 1992), *Raaz* (Bhatt, 2002), *Krishna Cottage* (Varma, 2004), *Eight: The Power of Shani* (Razdan, 2006), and *Darling* (Varma, 2007), which narrativize how destructive female desire can be. An examination of these films will reveal the nature of sexual differences, the nature of monstrosity in relation to gender, and the way the Hindi horror genre has represented the monstrous other feminine.

Mangalsutra and the Monstrous Other Feminine

As an archetypal monstrous-other-feminine narrative, *Mangalsutra* (Vijay, 1981) marks the inaugural moment of this subgenre even as it reiterates the Hindu tale of the mythical Savitri in a modernist mode and idealizes devotion and self-sacrifice to domesticity and patriarchy. Vijay (Anant Nag) and Gayatri (Rekha), betrothed to each other in childhood, are the progeny of best friends Badri Prasad (Madan Puri) and Mohan (Om Shivpuri). With their fate thus sealed by an oral contract between complicit paternities, the prefatory sequences are devoted to the building up of the lovers' courtship under the watchful gaze of the patriarchy. Gayatri's father, Badri Prasad, is privy to Vijay's audio-taped messages mailed to Gayatri. Mohan allows his son Vijay to stay at his prospective in-laws' home before marriage, contrary to normative Indian practice. And though Vijay has easy access to Gayatri, their interaction is regulated. Even a brazenly worded romantic love duet between the lovers is embarrassingly interrupted by the ever-watchful fathers, signifying the omnipresent patriarchal gaze.

The young couple acknowledge the untenability of desire outside conjugality and refrain from the 'forbidden'.

This placid romanticism of the couple, duly approved by the patriarchate, ends in marriage, but is unexpectedly interrupted on the wedding night by an evil spirit, whose encroachment upon the narrative had been heralded earlier by a series of inauspicious events: a buffalo[6] runs amok at Vijay's marriage procession, the sacred nuptial cord catches fire, and vermillion spills on to the ground. On the wedding night, Vijay's advances are put on hold by Gayatri's diffident reluctance. In the song sequence that follows, however, Gayatri amply demonstrates that she does not lack desire; rather, her ultra-femininity and demureness work as a female masquerade and a subtle sexual collusion with patriarchy. Her coyness is a ruse and her attempts at averting Vijay's gaze serve to disguise her forays into the realms of desire and look. Through Althusserian interpolation Gayatri constitutes herself as a subject, refraining from conferring her gaze on Vijay but inviting his look, as is clear when she preens before the mirror, aware that she is being looked at (Figure 4.8). In John Berger's terms, Gayatri becomes both the 'surveyor' and the 'surveyed' (Berger, 2008, p. 46).

Vijay is able to assert his sexuality only when Gayatri has partially renounced hers, and her pretence of a lack of desire allows Vijay to project his own. But the consummation is wrecked by Vijay's sudden collapse. This brief attack is the prelude to more serious victimization in the later scenes. His father rushes in without as much as a knock, signalling the panoptic patriarchy that is lingering somewhere off-screen, even at this moment of intimacy. Vijay is hospitalized. The first skirmish with the supernatural manifests itself when Vijay abandons his hospital bed at midnight and attempts to violate Gayatri. The ever-vigilant patriarchy averts marital rape and preserves the sanctity of marriage. Vijay is brought home, and the possession is conveniently ignored as a 'fit'. A seemingly recovered Vijay makes another attempt at

Figure 4.8: Gayatri (Rekha) looks into the mirror, aware that she is being looked at by Vijay (Anant Nag) in *Mangalsutra*.
Courtesy: Gaurav Films International, Madras.

intimacy, but when Gayatri chides him teasingly, 'First eat; if you don't … you will grow weak', her earlier masquerade of sexual naivety gives way in a Freudian slip. However, all sexual expectations are dissipated in the emphasis on Gayatri's nurturing abilities; she is rendered safe within the strictures of hegemonic gender divisions. Vijay, however, makes another forceful bid on Gayatri and is again duly thwarted by the patriarchy. An exorcism follows, crudely picturized as the writhing body of a woman superimposed on Vijay; Kamini (Prema Narayan) is introduced as the evil spirit with a tale to tell.

Two flashbacks follow in quick succession. In the first Kamini, speaking through Vijay alleges that possession is punishment for her rape by Vijay. The flashback takes viewers to a dark and stormy night during which Kamini, returning from a party, is waylaid by a band of hoodlums. Vijay rescues her from them but takes her to his home and then rapes her, promising marriage as consolation. The crime, perpetrated off-screen, is merely inferred by the audience from Kamini's desperate calls to Vijay for restraint. Later, two disembodied hands exchange rings, with the promise of marriage. Kamini says it was Vijay's betrayal that forced her to suicide. This flashback is a moment of crucial significance as it ruptures the narration, unhinges the audience's expectations, and introduces a notion of suspense. Vijay's fidelity, established so meticulously before, now appears suspect. Having apparently violated a prohibition, punishment for him appears legitimate.

With her vengeance 'legitimized' Kamini emerges as the all-powerful non-phallic symbol of sexuality and a nemesis of the male hero. Possession reduces Vijay to a state of powerlessness and enacts his symbolic castration; he is unable to consummate his marriage. Vijay's feminization and subjection to pain by the sadist Kamini become all the more obvious when he describes the onset of possession as 'penetration' (Figure 4.9).

An exorcism expels Kamini, albeit temporarily. Vijay recovers and now his redemptive flashback follows, which presents Kamini as the sexual aggressor while he is the victim of Kamini's threatening gaze and desire. A series of events from this flashback unfold on-screen: Kamini stalking Vijay in college; Kamini spreading rumours about their engagement, much to Vijay's chagrin; and, finally, Vijay returning home one day to find Kamini in his bedroom. As he spurns her advances an impromptu striptease song is played out.

A subjective panning camera shot appropriating Vijay's gaze first brings Kamini's floral-patterned and colourful undergarments into the frame and then Kamini herself sprawled invitingly on his bed, wrapped in a towel. Throughout the song sequence that follows Vijay struggles

...and I feel as if someone was penetrating my body.

Figure 4.9: Vijay describing possession by the monstrous 'other' feminine as symbolic penetration in *Mangalsutra*.
Courtesy: Gaurav Films International, Madras.

to gain a visual foothold in Kamini's presence while she gazes at him unabashedly. Significantly enough, when Vijay looks at Kamini, his gaze is appropriated by subjective camera shots, fetishizing Kamini. When Kamini 'appropriates the look', we see her looking at Vijay through objective shots that spare male heterosexual spectators' the trauma of experiencing the objectification of the male body through the female gaze (Figure 4.10).

Minor but significant details also substantiate the differences between the repressed sexuality of the domesticated wife Gayatri, whose femininity is singled out through visual markers such as her *sari* and *sindoor*, and the casual and unrestrained facets of Kamini's sexuality, expressed through items of her apparel. She wears a split-to-the-thigh gown that reflects her sexual openness. Through disavowal and repulsion, Vijay thwarts her feelers and hits out at her

Figure 4.10: The camera frames Kamini (Prema Narayan) looking at Vijay (Anant Nag), who looks away from her. A scene from Vijay's flashback in *Mangalsutra*. *Courtesy:* Gaurav Films International, Madras.

in an act of final rejection. Kamini storms out in a rage and dies in a road accident thereafter.

Vijay's narrative is authenticated over Kamini's through the presence of an alibi. Vijay's friend (Shashi Puri) attests to Kamini's uninhibited desire and assures the audience of Vijay's fidelity. With this substantiation, Kamini's narrative of being a victim of rape is falsified and the *raison d'être* of revenge is delegitimized. 'The projection onto others of one's own repressed desires constitutes the classic mechanism of paranoia' (Williams, 1981). Kamini's self-identification as the victim becomes a paranoid projection, her misplaced sense of victimhood merely an outward projection of her own corrupt, debased passion.

As Vijay is repossessed and condemned to die, Gayatri rushes to pray to the Lord Shiva, symbol of male creative energy. Though Hindu iconography often depicts Shiva as *Ardhanārīśvara*, one half of the body male and the other female; 'the most basic and most common object of worship in Shiv shrines is the phallus or lingam' (Zimmer, 1992, p. 126). The climax conflates divinity and masculinity. Invoked through her prayers, the deity manifests his third eye and destroys the usurper of the gaze. Towards the denouement, the mythical Savitri is refigured through Gayatri, who saves her husband from death and restores the patriarchy. The film upholds the untenability of autonomous female desire outside conjugality and asserts the primacy of patriarchal law.

An examination of the competing femininities of Gayatri and Kamini has much to offer. The more they fight over Vijay, the more the differences between them get erased. Gayatri and Kamini are alike in that they are both committed to go to any length to possess the man they desire. But whereas Gayatri's sexuality, hedged within the sanctity of marriage, is deified as exemplary, Kamini's invites censure and divine retribution. As a subject sutured into patriarchy, Gayatri gains social acceptability and the audience's sympathy. Within the traditional sexual economies of exchange, the appropriating gaze must remain the prerogative of the male subject, but Kamini not only possesses the gaze, she aggressively courts it, as the threatening sexual 'other' can be rejected only through denunciation and disavowal. Gayatri looking away from Vijay on her wedding night is accordingly an acute internalization of the patriarchal order.

The 'aversion of gaze' and 'disavowal of desire' are skills that enable Gayatri's entrée into the patriarchal order, in the way that projecting women as 'non-sexual' entities facilitated their entry into the outside world in colonial times. Gayatri's love does not appear spontaneous. With her match fixed at birth, Gayatri's desire for Vijay is but a 'patriarchal obligation'. Kamini's sexuality, on the other hand, is a matter of choice. Again, while Gayatri is introduced in the film through a photograph which Vijay carries on his person to be able to bestow his 'gaze' on her, Gayatri has 'surrendered' her gaze and prefers to listen to Vijay on audio tapes. The mangal sutra also 'queers' the pitch and possession becomes a queer act with homosexual overtones. Gayatri's heterosexuality stands in contrast to Kamini's excursions into suspected lesbianism: if Kamini experiences pain through Vijay's body during an exorcism, we are to assume that she receives pleasure when Vijay attempts to violate Gayatri.

With star image as the reference point, the casting of Prema Narayan as Kamini and Rekha as the pious wife Gayatri reaffirms spectatorial conventions. Exorcism through divine intercessions not only expels the monstrous other feminine but also punishes the female body for unrestrained desire and gaze. Kamini is disavowed and annihilated symbolically through a phallic *trishul* (trident) that penetrates her ethereal body, and this moment marks her de-phallicization.

The conscious/cultural prevails over the biological/instinctual. Gendered order is restored, the status quo is reaffirmed. The rational–secular Vijay, who had earlier denounced divinity, returns to the 'fold of faith' and the film ends with a freeze frame of *Shivling*. Kamini's cultural 'Otherness' possibly as an Anglo-Indian is implied but never explicitly stated with finality, yet her gravestone in a 'cemetery' hardly leaves room for doubt about Kamini's non-Hindu identity. While Gayatri's sexuality may be repressed it is this repressed sexuality that is deified in *Mangalsutra's* narrative. *Mangalsutra* anticipates the similarity of structured narratives of the later films in the following decade.

Veerana

Kamini's desire and threatening gaze in *Mangalsutra* (Vijay, 1981) is displaced on to the witch Nikita, the avenging monstrous other feminine in *Veerana* (Ramsay & Ramsay, 1988), a film that explicitly identifies female desire as socially corrupting and mortally threatening. Nikita preys upon men, both sexually and otherwise. Sameer Pratap (Vijayendra Ghatge) entraps the witch and strings her up, but he is abducted by Nikita's avenging worshippers, and her soul is made to enter his teenaged niece Jasmine (Jasmin). In his absence Sameer Pratap is presumed dead by his family. Years go by and an adult Jasmine grows up to prey upon men in a licentious fashion similar to Nikita's. The tight cinematic framing of Jasmine's body in her introductory shots offers an abundant display of fetishism, signifying the fear of female sexuality, but through objectification *Veerana* recuperates wounded masculinity. Jasmine is introduced through a double structure of 'look'; a striptease song plays as she is framed in a woman-at-the-keyhole moment which demystifies her. We appropriate the 'look' of the servant spying on her through a keyhole, whose gaze we are invited to share (Figure 4.11).

Figure 4.11: A woman-in-a-keyhole moment imparts a voyeuristic gaze to the viewer in *Veerana.*
Courtesy: Sai Om Productions.

The camera then abandons the pretence of the surreptitious gaze and transplants the viewer directly into Jasmine's bathing chamber. Her seductive dancing becomes a privatized striptease for the male viewer and, at one point, Jasmine breaks the fourth wall to look directly at the spectator. The camera vengefully re-enacts a misogynist dismemberment of the female form. Jasmine's threatening sexuality is overpowered through voyeurism as the camera fetishizes her body, lingers on her legs, exposed midriff, cleavage, bare back. Throughout the song, close-up shots ignore the illusion of screen depth and symbolically mutilate and dismember her body.

The narrative crisis is precipitated by Jasmine's attempts to steal another woman's man, Hemant (Hemant Birje), the boyfriend of her cousin Sahila (Sahila Chaddha). But the long-missing patriarch Sameer Pratap returns in the nick of time to save the hetero-normative relationship. An entrapped Nikita released within the hallowed precincts of a Shiva temple disintegrates under the divine *darshanic* gaze. Like Kamini in *Mangalsutra,* Nisha (Dimple Kapadia) the monstrous other feminine in *Bees Saal Baad* (Kohli, 1988) desirous of Kiran's (Meenakshi Sheshadri) husband Suraj (Mithun Chakraborty), seeks to imbricate herself in a monogamous relationship and her gaze becomes the means through which she exercises orphic powers to move things, levitate objects and enchant and enamour Suraj towards herself (Figure 4.12). Suraj goes into a trance whenever under Nisha's gaze. Mithun Chakraborty, who played macho roles in most of his films, appears as less than an inspiring figure of virility, when subjected to female desire and gaze.

Suryavanshi (Kumar, 1992) shares major narrative complicities with the construction of the monstrous femininity of *Mangalsutra* and is about the centuries old ghost of Princess Suryalekha (Amrita Singh) who seeks a (sexual) reunion with the much-married Vicky (Salman Khan). Like Gayatri in *Mangalsutra,* Sonia (Sheeba) is Vicky's sacrificing wife in an arranged match fixed by colluding patriarchies.

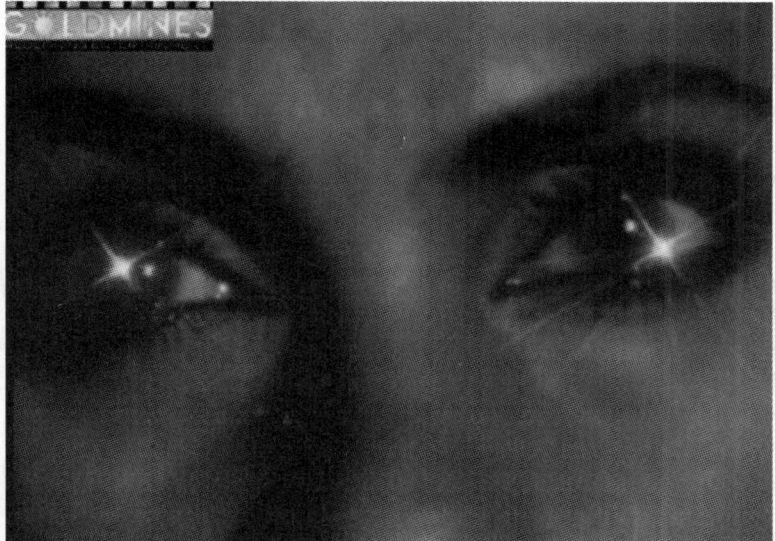

Figure 4.12: Nisha's gaze is the means through which she exercises most of her orphic powers including enamouring the married Suraj towards herself in *Bees Saal Baad*.
Courtesy: Geetanjali Pictures.

Suryalekha in *Suryavanshi* is Kamini of *Mangalsutra*, spatially 'dislocated' onto another time–space plane. Like the avenging spirit of Kamini in *Mangalsutra*, Suryalekha is a veritable castrating nemesis who would symbolically emasculate her suitors by challenging them to mortal duels. Suryalekha is blatantly sexual, as her desire appears far more resilient, which can lay dormant for centuries. On the other hand, Sonia offers non-threatening affection, despite a consummation-less marriage to Vicky, who experiences sickness when Suryalekha's overpowering gaze falls upon him underlining the debilitating effect of the female controlling gaze. Exorcism in the climax reaffirms the normative status quo. In *Ek Thi Daayan* (Iyer, 2013) the witch Diana (Konkona Dev Sen) literally becomes the 'other' woman in Bobo's (Emraan Hashmi) life as she charms Bobo's widowed father and marries him.

This Foucauldian 'disciplining' of female desire in *Mangalsutra, Veerana* and later monstrous-other-feminine discourses such as *Bees Saal Baad* (Kohli, 1988), *Woh Phir Aayegi* (Ishaara, 1988), *Suryavanshi* (Kumar, 1992), *Zakhmi Rooh* (Kumar, 1993) does not appear arbitrary because it operates through the mechanism of divine justice and is free of guilt. In true Bakhtinian fashion of dialogism the Hindi horror cinema turns Hollywood's monstrous feminine into the monstrous 'other' feminine, the non-mother, monstrous sexual other, a castrating nemesis and mortal threat to patriarchal authority. With their narrative codes of wayward female sexuality and divine punishment through exorcism in the denouement, *Mangalsutra* and *Veerana* distinctly delineate the general thematic structures of similarly organized pre-liberalization monstrous-other-feminine narratives. But since hegemony is never stable this patriarchal hegemonic discourse must accommodate the counter-narrative discourse. Thus post-liberalization monstrous-other-feminine narratives such as *Raaz* (Bhatt, 2002), *Krishna Cottage* (Varma, 2004), *Eight: The power of Shani* (Razdan, 2006) and *Darling* (Varma, 2007) reiterate the same destructiveness of uninhibited female desire but appear conciliatory and renegotiate more novel terms of submission as I shall demonstrate.

Modernization of Patriarchy and Post-liberalization Female Monstrosity

By the 1980s, the state's initiative in recognizing sexual harassment, female claim over legislative representations, gendered neutrality in the workplace, acknowledgement of hitherto live-in relations, promotion of female reproductive rights, and the state-sponsored family planning programmes' bid to control population through the birth control pill placed the womenfolk at the centre of its campaigns, which imperilled entrenched patriarchal values and yielded massive gender confusion in the 1990s. With liberalization in the 1990s, India embarked upon a knowledge-based economy, and workplaces began to exhibit gender diversity. The Indian public sphere witnessed a proliferation of erotic visuals, heralded by a series of print advertisements for Kamasutra condoms, which focused 'unequivocally if not solely on erotic pleasure ... and foreground[ed] the erotic desires and pleasures of the woman' (Mankekar, 2004, p. 415). This sexualization of Indian television took place in the context of 'feverish commodity consumption precipitated by the expansion of mass culture, the liberalization of the Indian economy and the introduction of global capital' (Mankekar, 2004, p. 408). Television re-fashioned social habits and consumption patterns. With the feminization of the workplace, cinema stretched its demographics to the new constituency of a recent upwardly mobile female spectatorship, lately empowered through economic reforms. As Bakhtin writes, 'utterance is constructed while taking into account possible responsive reactions, for whose sake in essence it is actually created' (Bakhtin, 1986, p. 94) and to conciliate dominant cultural anxieties engineered by the media industry's somewhat blatant explications of female desire; patriarchal surveillance was remoulded in the subgenre to accommodate the female gaze.

Marking genre anxiety, a moment of conflict between 'conservative continuity reinforced by the persistence of generic forms and the ceaseless pattern of social change' (Lipsitz, 1998, p. 209), the monstrous-other-feminine subgenre moved away from the essentialist position of compulsory repression of female sexual autonomy to a more revisionist discourse that sought to reappraise female sexuality/desire in more considerate terms and offered the male body for uninhibited female scopophilic gaze. Panoptic patriarchal gaze so evident in *Mangalsutra*, *Bees Saal Baad*, *Veerana*, *Suryavanshi* acquires invisibility in later films. The post-liberalization narratives impart a quasi-legitimacy to these monstrous other females softening their evilness and investing them with a cause that invites the audience's sympathy. Their narrative closures do away with the need to exorcise the 'monstrous other feminine' in the dénouement, as in *Krishna Cottage* (Varma, 2004), *Eight: The power of Shani* (Razdan, 2006), *Darling* (Varma, 2007) and *Click* (Sivan, 2010).

Raaz

As a revisionist horror narrative marking a substantial shift in the narrative strategies of the subgenre *Raaz* (Bhatt, 2002) tenders several opportunities for male objectification and announces the introduction of the female gaze, offering the quintessential metrosexual male lead Aditya (Dino Morea) for female scopophilic consumption (Figures 4.13 and 4.14).

A newly-married Aditya, alone on a business trip to Ooty, is accosted by the mysterious, footloose Malini (Malini Sharma) and is seduced by her. When the affair subsides,

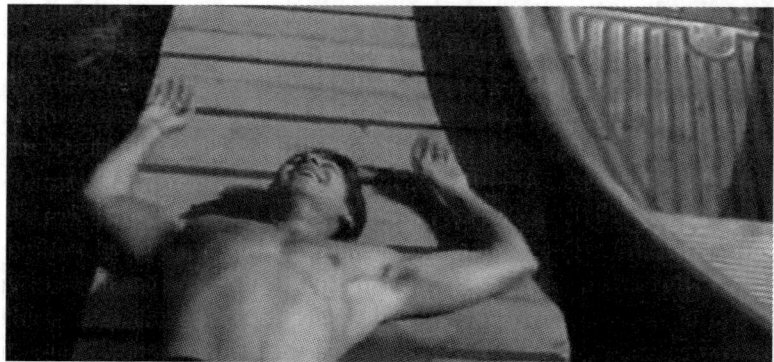

Figure 4.13: A subjective camera appropriates Sanjana's gaze marking the reversal of the 'look' and the objectification of the male body in *Raaz* . *Courtesy:* Bhatt Productions.

Figure 4.14: Sanjana's look (Bipasha Basu) as she savours the moment of the female gaze in *Raaz*.
Courtesy: Bhatt Productions.

Aditya's refusal to divorce his wife and acknowledge Malini's presence beyond the bedroom leads her to commit suicide. Fearing the law, Malini's body is secretly buried and Aditya returns home, but the traumatic event leaves him 'limp' and 'unmanned', marking the loss of libido and his symbolic emasculation, precipitating the narrative crisis with which the film's plot opens.

Malini's voyeuristic presence, implied through point-of-view shots, intrudes upon and disrupts the couple's intimacy, just as Kamini's presence had dampened passions in *Mangalsutra* (Vijay, 1981). Kept in abeyance, Malini's spectral presence is ushered into the narrative, and the transiently possessed Sanjana extracts a confession. Aditya admits to his 'reluctant' sexual transgression but it was the neurotically obsessed Malini, he implies, who had initiated the extramarital relationship.

As a mere accomplice to this transgression, Aditya stands exonerated, and patriarchy is absolved. A transition to an earlier event through a flashback interrupts the chronological development of the story and the solo song *aapke pyaar main* (in your love), shows Malini as a dominatrix and wielder of the phallus. An unclothed Aditya is propped against a tree while Malini goes all over him. In the climax, however, the monstrous phallus-appropriating femininity of Malini is banished once again, and Sanjana battles to save her husband's life and the marriage. *Krishna Cottage* endows the traditional institution of marriage with repelling power and therapeutic abilities strong enough to repulse malefic forces and impart the lead couple Manav and Shanti with spiritual protection. Disha (Isha Koppikar) the monstrous 'Other' feminine can be repelled only if Manav ties the sacred nuptial cord with his girlfriend Shanti, since 'marriage in Hindu rituals transcends time and birth and will bind their destiny together'. In a sentimentalized epilogue, the marriage is socialized and sanctified, emerging as an antidote to a vicious obsessed *pret atma*. The key makeover in the conclusion is not the transformation of Disha into a more considerate evil spirit but that of the exuberant and sexual Shanti who comes out in the opening sequence in a swim suit, through an 'in your face' MTV style fun and frolicking song sequence.

Eight: The Power of Shani

As another revisionist attempt, *Eight: The Power of Shani* (Razdan, 2006) seeks to assuage feminist anxieties and concerns but offers multiple points of contacts with the tralatitious order. Set in London, the family of patriarch Suraj Rai (Gulshan Grover) experiences mysterious malefic paranormal activity in their home on Saturdays and on dates that total eight, the number attributed to the Hindu deity *Shani*.[7] A mysterious apparition of a woman in red appears to be keeping a watchful gaze on the family members. A terrified Rai flees with his family and like Aditya's cathartic moment in *Raaz*, owns up to a fling with Kamini (Vastavikta), an ardent worshipper of *Shani*. A generic flashback establishes Kamini's wayward sexuality and Suraj's trepid complicity.

Suraj promises marriage to Kamini but later explains away the relationship as transient and purely functional. 'I have a wife and daughter', he reasons. Aware of Suraj's predicament, Kamini asks Suraj to marry her anyway: 'Marry me, and I won't stop you from visiting your family'. The densely layered presence of numerous discourses all aligned against secular modernity converge upon this crucial moment. Bigamy is a statutory offence in England and the Wales where the story is set. In India, Nehruvian reforms outlawed bigamy for Hindus. Hindi cinema routinely resolves the dilemma of bigamy through the ritual extermination of the second female lead.

When the promised marriage does not materialize, a traumatized Kamini, unable to transubstantiate her pleasure principle into reality pleasure, drives off a cliff and dies. In Freudian interpretation, the erotic instinct and the desire for death are fused together. From desire to death, Kamini moves from Eros to Thanatos and returns to haunt the family. Kamini's suicide turns her into an avenging monstrous other feminine, but one whose actions stand consecrated through divine fiat. A number of questions in this particular sequence are not accounted for. What animates the deity *Shani* on Kamini's behalf when Kamini with her (im)morality and sexual transgression is not precisely the paragon of traditional virtuousness? What sanctifies Kamini's revenge?

First, if the divine punishment inflicted on Suraj is for sexual transgression then both Kamini and Suraj are equally guilty of dishonouring the sacrosanctity of monogamous Hindu marriage. Second, the divinity is not expecting Suraj to dissolve his marriage with his wife Radha (Padmini Kolhapure) for that would be equally immoral and undermine the divinity's claim at evenhandedness. Third, divinity has not sided with Kamini merely because she is a worshipper of *Shani*, for that presents divinity as biased and inclined to favouritism. Once all the probable hypotheses for divine chastisement on Rai are invalidated what remains is his dishonoured promise of marriage to Kamini. So what kind of spousal relationship is Kamini demanding when she does not want Suraj to divorce his first wife? Kamini is demanding a marriage that the modernist/secularist discourse has disavowed but which classical Hinduism[8] honours and recognizes. Although the second wife's legal tenability is disavowed by the modernist Nehruvian discourse it has precedence in Hinduism that existed prior to the introduction of Nehruvian reforms. Only on Suraj's outright rejection of *this* possibility that Kamini drives off to her death and elicits divine retribution to work for her rather than against her. Kamini exists in two different planes: the secular–historical Kamini who is aware of Suraj's marital status, bound as he is to secular laws that have 'criminalized' bigamy; the ahistorical–mythical Kamini, believer in the powers of *Shani*, and the immutability of divine jurisprudence. In the denouement it is to this Kamini that Rai surrenders and seeks forgiveness. In compliance with the conventions of the genre, the 'Other' woman Kamini retreats and the monogamous heteronormative coupledom is re-established.

The narrative subverts the desacralized laws and the inviolability of the monogamous relationship sanctioned by the late post-colonial secular state. However, in the climax the law of marriage overwhelms desire and Eros submits to cultural constraints. Marking a not-so-subtle change of divine posturing, Kamini is divinely 'allowed' to punish Suraj. This is a remarkable change from the divinity of *Mangalsutra* which had penalized Kamini (Prema Narayan) under similar circumstances. *Eight: The Power of Shani* therefore presents an ever-evolving divinity and exposes the deficiency of manmade 'secular' laws that ignore the possibilities of human relations. *Eight: The Power of Shani* (Razdan, 2006) also assuages anxieties about *Shani*, a celestial body often looked upon with fear and dread from among the Hindu pantheons and bestows upon it the benignancy of the more restrained Hindu divinities. In quotidian Hindu practices *Shani* is either to be avoided or appeased. In the denouement, Suraj seeks forgiveness from both Kamini and *Shani Maharaj* and is shown praying at *Shani Shingnapur* in Maharashtra, an important shrine for Lord *Shani*.

Darling

A divinity that recognizes female sexuality heralding the forging of a new alliance, as we shall see, resurfaces in *Darling* (Varma, 2007). *Darling* (Varma, 2007) rescripts the monstrous narrative and showcases the active sexuality of the vengeful spirit Geeta (Esha Deol), who is allowed to conquer the passivity of the wife Ashwini (Isha Koppikar). Aditya (Fardeen Khan) has an extramarital relationship with his secretary Geeta, but it flounders on the broken promise of marriage. They fight during an amorous rendez-vous, and Geeta is accidentally killed. She returns from the dead as the monstrous other feminine, her gaze perpetually fixed on Aditya. As a post-liberalization *femme castratrice*, her specular surveillance is limited to embarrassing Aditya and dampening things in the bedroom, which again can be read as symbolic castration (Figure 4.15).

But Geeta's monstrosity is also a dilution of evilness. As a ghost she can visit the temple and seek divine inter-vention on her behalf. The patriarchal gaze, so panoptic in *Mangalsutra* (1981), becomes invisible in *Darling* (2007), and despite the absence of a patriarchate in the nuclear house-hold, the restrained eroticism and modesty of Aditya's domesticated wife (Koppikar) is but the internalization of patriarchal surveillance. She takes to policing herself, as when she looks visibly embarrassed when Aditya offers her a foot massage. Like *Mangalsutra*'s Gayatri, Ashwini is wedded to sexual modesty. If Geeta had enjoyed a foot massage, Ashwini looks embarrassed when offered one by Aditya. She remains confined within the four walls of

Figure 4.15: Geeta's specular surveillance (shown in center) disrupts conjugal intimacy between Aditya (Fardeen Khan) and his wife Ashwini (left) in *Darling*. *Courtesy:* Super Cassettes Industries Limited (T-Series).

domesticity and her access to public spaces is chaperoned by her husband. Her only outing with Aditya is to the friendly neighbourhood single theatre and a shopping mall. Meanwhile, Geeta's body is subjected to a fetishized representation, with the camera appropriating the male gaze, lingering on Geeta's derrière in one scene. But as a genre-revisionist narrative, *Darling* not only offers benignancy to Geeta's ghost, the camera also identifies with Geeta's gaze, objectifying the male body by offering the audience a glimpse of Aditya's crotch (Figure 4.16).

The controversial climax reintegrates Geeta with domesticity as the wife dies in an accident, and her body is taken over by the paramour. Geeta's amorous desire is neither suppressed nor returned but rather legitimized and sublimated into Ashwini's body, quite literally. Far from being expelled violently from the narrative, she is accommodated within the coupledom left open by the wife's death.

If the 'final girl'[9] who survives and defeats the killer/monster is phallicized and given masculine traits in Hollywood's monstrous-feminine narratives, Gayatri (Rekha)

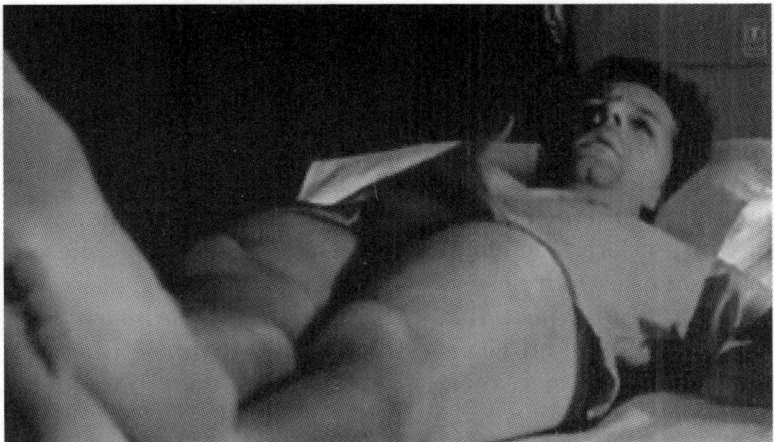

Figure 4.16: As post-liberalization monstrous 'Other' feminine narrative, *Darling* offers a peek at male objectification through female gaze as in this shot which shows Aditya in his underthings.
Courtesy: Super Cassettes Industries Limited (T-Series).

in *Mangalsutra*, Kiran (Meenakshi Sheshadri) in *Bees Saal Baad*, Aarti (Farah) in *Woh Phir Aayegi*, Sonia (Sheeba) in *Suryavanshi*, Reema (Moon Moon Sen) in *Zakhmi Rooh*, Sanjana (Bipasha Basu) in *Raaz*, Shanti (Anita Hassandani) in *Krishna Cottage* and Ashwini (Isha Koppikar) in *Darling* are artificialities, camouflages and masquerades, designed to cover desire and discount the reprisals that possessing desire would invite. The pretence of sexual naivety serves to conceal a femininity that dare not speak its desire. On the other hand, the wives, whether it is Gayatri in *Mangalsutra* who inadvertently reveals her sexual self in a Freudian slip, or Sonia in *Suryavanshi* who can transform into a *femme* fatale for a seductive song sequence, or Aarti who becomes sexual in *Woh Phir Aayegi*, are not allowed to stray too far from the norm of patriarchal discourse. Through self-authored marginalization, normative femininity induces them to assume subordinate positions within patriarchic narratives, signalling disempowerment that wifehood signifies in the cultural frames offered in the films. But nonetheless they save themselves from the certain annihilation to which Kamini (*Mangalsutra*), Nisha (*Bees Saal Baad*), Nikita (*Veerana*), Seema (*Zakhmi Rooh*) Suryalekha (*Suryavanshi*), and Malini (*Raaz*) are subjected. Transgressive women die; restrained women live to tell the tale.

With the destruction/expulsion of the monstrous other feminine from the narrative, the final girl is the woman who has surrendered her claim to desire and gaze and acquiesces in passive sexuality.

Even though *Jadu Tona* (Nagaich, 1977), *Gehrayee* (Raje & Desai, 1980) and *Gauri* (Akbar, 2007) feature pubescent female adolescents, there is a powerful invitation to re-transcribe them as analogous to monstrous other feminine. In *Jadu Tona*, the young Harsha undergoes spells of possession whenever she hurts herself and 'bleeds', symbolically signifying menstruation and female sexuality. Harsha's bleeding body is the only visible monster in *Jadu Tona*. With bleeding and possession occurring simultaneously, her supernatural powers and superhuman strengths become a literal transcription of her sexuality. Exorcism not only dispossesses the evil spirit of Harsha it also successfully navigates her back to the non-threatening innocence of pre-pubescent adolescence.

In *Gehrayee*, possession marks Uma's transition from a state of sexual ignorance to uninhibited sexual frankness; Uma imbricates herself circuitously in the marital relationship of her parents by revealing torrid details of her father's one-night stand and engenders a parental marital crisis. She returns to sexual sobriety once the exorcism expels the evil spirit from within. Whereas *Gauri: The Unborn* (Akbar, 2007) has been read as undermining female reproductive liberty and 'dissolution of modernity' (Sen, 2011) and presents the tale of an aborted fetus' retribution *to* coerce its parents into acknowledging their guilt by threatening to carry out an act of sororicide. Yet another reading is possible, and the sub-texts within the film can produce multiple and complimentary interpretations. When possessed by the aborted foetus, the teen daughter Shivani (Rushita Pandya) becomes Gauri, the monstrous other feminine, a seething mass of spectral rage who suffers bouts of jealously and is willing to commit an act of sororicide beyond what even a dubious notion of vengeance can justify. Her vengeance can be transcribed in Freudian terms. Her single-minded attacks on her mother alone present an unrealized Electra complex and point to unresolved incestuous desire. When possessed by Gauri, the adolescent Shivani wants to sleep in her parents' bed, spies upon and disrupts their intimate moments.

Julius Lipner asserts that in the classical Hindu per-spective, the embryo enjoys a special status and deserves protection. Hindu *dharma sastras* (holy texts) prescribe the same punishment for killing a Brahmin and a pregnant woman, and abortion is unacceptable because it interferes with the life cycles of birth and rebirth as abortion removes a person's chance to be born and work towards achieving the goal of *moksha* or liberation (Lipner, 1989, p. 4). Similarly, Islam considers abortion as haram or prohibited, permis-sible only under extraordinary circumstances. Specific Koranic verses[10] extol the faithful not to kill offspring for fear of poverty. *Gauri*'s narration is intended to induce post-abortion guilt, and its dominant discourse is to undermine women's reproductive rights instead of letting a woman negotiate motherhood on her terms. As Irina Lester enjoins: 'Forcing a woman to become a mother against her wishes comes from the same place as banning her from opening a bank account in her name or excluding her from the right to vote' (Lester, 2007). Like Vijay's courtship in *Mangalsutra* carried out under the panoptical patriarchal gaze, in *Gauri* the patriarch (Anupam Kher), Sudeep's father privy to the couple's decision to abort the fetus, intrusively admon-ishes the engaged couple for not being 'too careful', and denies their right to be discreet. Ignoring even the most quintessentially legitimate reason of a woman not to bear pregnancy *Gauri* demands that motherhood be borne even when it is forced and undesired. Sexual activity in *Gauri* is in contravention of the strict economy of tradition, because its object is not procreation. In this sense *Gauri* prescribes motherhood as a destiny for every sexual act.

The monstrous-other-feminine subgenre of Hindi horror cinema hovers between conservative nostalgia and images of feminine autonomy, exciting assertiveness and defensive posturing and offers female desire and look which is condemned either to discipline or annihilation. The monstrous other feminine is a phallic woman one moment and a fetishized woman the next. When entrusted with this gaze of female objectification, the female spectator writes Mary Anne Doane can adopt, 'the masochism of over identification' or the narcissism entailed in becoming one's own object of desire' (Smelik, 1999, p. 357). The female spectator can become complicit in the male gaze, through appropriation of Mulveyian 'to be looked at ness' (Mulvey, 1989, p. 19). Alternately, she may appropriate the homoerotic gaze and become her own object of desire. As part of a dynamic patriarchal discourse, the monstrous-other-feminine narrative of Hindi horror cinema anticipates and accommodates the counter-hegemonic dialogue. The appropriation of gaze and desire by the monstrous other feminine opens up a space of resistance but within the limits set by patriarchy. Thus, an exploration of the cinematic subjectivities reveals that 'specific historical moment[s] ha[ve] affected the Hindi horror genre' (Mubarki, 2013, p. 60) and the monstrous narratives enmesh the fear of the interstitial phantasmal female within the larger framework of cultural misogyny and patriarchal fear of the all-powerful feminine.

Notes

1. See Koran Chapter 113, Verses 1–4: Say I seek refuge with the Lord of the rising day… from the evil of the women who blow on knots.
2. For more on the science debates of the 1980s, see (Nanda, 1998).

3. While the gaze is impersonal and ubiquitous, the look is the desiring act of an eye seeing just one viewpoint (Heffernan, 1997, p. 138).
4. Interestingly enough Indrani Sen speaks of similar cultural mobilization and preoccupation with femininity was evident in the exhortatory writings in British Anglo Indian writings of the period which focused 'on the moral responsibilities of the English women in India' See Indrani Sen (2002).
5. Deborah Jermyn describes the 'bitches from hell' as 'women whose violence, cunning and monstrosity are almost unparalleled in the women who form their cinematic predecessors' (Jermyn, 1996, p. 251).
6. Hindu mythological iconography presents the buffalo as a portent for either death or evil. Yama, the god of death, is often shown seated on a buffalo, and the Hindu goddess Durga is often presented slaying Mahishasura, the buffalo demon. The word *mahisha* is Sanskrit for 'buffalo'.
7. *Shani* (Saturn) is one of the nine primary celestial bodies in Hindu mythology, as well as the elder brother of the Hindu god of death, Yama. If Yama awards punishment after death, *Shani* metes out the result of deeds 'while alive on the earth' (Rajasthani, 2006, p. 9).
8. I define Classical Hinduism as one that existed prior to the reform initiated through the Hindu Marriage Act of 1955.
9. I borrow the term 'final girl' from Carol Clover to refer to the female hero who appropriates the role of the male lead in vanquishing the monster (Clover, 1992, p. 260) such as Laurie Strode (Jamie Lee) in *Halloween* (Carpenter, 1978), Alice (Adrienne King) in *Friday the 13th* (Cunningham, 1980), Tracy Harris (Jennifer Jason Leigh) in *Eyes of a Stranger* (Wiederhorn, 1981) and Nancy Thompson (Heather Langenkamp) in *A Nightmare on Elm Street* (Craven, 1984).
10. See Koran verse 17:32.

5

The Inflection of the Hindutva 'Ideo'logic Cinema

In the final moments of *Bandh Darwaza* (Ramsay & Ramsay, 1990), Neola (Anirudh Agarwal), the vampire, returning from his nightly raid enters his lair and is about to secrete himself into his coffin when he suddenly sees that his casket now houses a strategically placed cross inside. Strongly repulsed by some invisible 'radiation' emanating from it, he stumbles back, even as the chimes of bells of church are heard extra-deigetically, and the camera abruptly cuts to an extreme close-up of a crucified Christ. In desperation, Neola moves towards another casket and finds an open Koran with the sound of the *azan* in the background — a cutaway shot places the book centrally within the frame (Figure 5.1).

Repulsed, the monster lurches towards his tormentor only to be beaten back by an *Om* insignia held up like a cross and the sound of the blowing of the *shankhs* (conch shells) signalling the final confrontation between good and evil. But if all faiths appear affective in repelling evil, no faith is allowed to lay singular claim in annihilating it. In an austere representation of fair play, Neola's destruction is wrought through a non-sectarian act; the repository of his malevolent soul, a statue, is burnt to the ground and the monster is vanquished. The film *Bandh Darwaza* (Ramsay

Figure 5.1: The cutaway shot of a Koran inside the coffin of Vampire Neola (Anirudh Agarwal) in *Bandh Darwaza*.
Courtesy: Ramsay Productions.

and Ramsay, 1990) was released at a time of the general decline of Centrist politics and the emergence of Hindutva polemics in India.

Around the late 1980s, as Bhrigupati Singh notes, relaxed import duties allowed private Indian companies to obtain distribution rights of foreign films bypassing the representatives of Hollywood studios—one had to negotiate a foreign exchange transaction through the government-controlled National Film Development Corporation (NFDC) and exhibition certification from the Central Board of Film Certification (CBFC) (Singh, 2008). With its 'for adult viewing only' certification, that placed it out of bounds for 'family audiences', a euphemism for women and children, the horror genre with titles such as *Aadamkhor* (Man Eater) (Shelly, 1986) and *Pyaasi Aatma* (Thirsty Soul) (Inamdar & Misra, 1988) found its place within exhibition centres noted for foreign and indigenous soft porn. However, by the early 1990s, the middle-class consumerist culture was

gaining ascendency and slowly dismantling the protection-
ist Nehruvian State. Desire and expression of the middle
class came to acquire urgent expressiveness, and consumption was increasingly being looked as a meaningful site for
identity where 'viewers believed that acquiring the goods
advertised on *Doordarshan* was essential to their ascend-
ance to middle class status' (Mankekar, 1999, p. 52). Middle
classness prefaced the middle class. What constituted
middle classness was not just 'toiletries, packaged food ...
but rather a sense of being that cannot be imparted through
ownership of vulgar commodities' (Shrivastava, 2007,
p. 243). As Sangita Gopal notes, 'immediately after the liberalization the Hindi horror suddenly went upscale recasting
itself as a metropolitan product addressed to India's glo-
balizing middle classes' (Gopal, 2011, p. 91). The gentrifica-
tion engendered by economic liberalization was reflected in
the urban renewal programmes in metropolitan landscapes
and the upper class reassertions of claims over public spaces
through construction of parks, inner-city recreational centres and multiplexes. Nothing symbolized this more than the
decline of single-theatre exhibition systems and the concurrent rise of the multiplexes in posh spheres of the Indian
metropolises, which became both a symptom and symbol
of newly emergent consuming values. The Ramsays disap-
peared into this cusp of dissolving single theatres and the
concurrent rise of the multiplexes, resurfacing in television
through their Zee Horror show series (1993–1998), suitably
neutered for middle-class drawing room sensitivities.

Within the particular discourses of the politics of taste
that developed in post-liberalization India, which allowed
social classes to either maintain or improve upon their
social standing by pursuing strategies where economic
capital was transmuted or exchanged for cultural capital, the Ramsays were devalued and delegitimized and
deemed trashy by the 'respectable' film culture and critical discourse of film evaluation. With their explicitness as
part of the self-avowed aesthetics of supererogatory gore

and sex, the Ramsay Brothers' production house eschewed aspirational respectability of middle classness to which the Indian middle class was aspiring. Unlike the horror films of Ram Gopal Verma who made his entry into the genre with *Raat*, the monstrous presence in a Ramsay production does not lurk somewhere off the frame. Instead, its very bearing and blatant presence is established and imposed early on in the narrative. The monster/ghost in a generic Ramsay production is a fully constituted ontological presence brought forth not by any suicide or murder or unperformed last rites. It commands a prior existence. Visual blatancy leaves no room for cognitive uncertainty and with no delayed collective social confirmation in the denouement, the camera does not shy away from the monster, it fetishizes it. The monster's all too physical presence is there for all to see and acknowledge. Overdetermined by this aesthetic strategy, the Ramsays' style demands full visibility within the overarching discourse of excess of melodrama as expounded by Peter Brooks and defined as, 'the effect of the mode's fundamental drive towards "expressivity": the "desire to express all", "to utter the unspeakable" [which] produces an excess of meaning in defiance of social and psychic repression' (Gillman, 2003, p. 16). Compared to the modernist emphasis on the unavailability and unreliableness of reality, 'melodrama was 'an outdated and embarrassingly crude approach to the problem of artistic mimesis which the realistic mode ... had managed to overcome and leave behind' (Kelleter & Mayer, 2007, p. 10). Melodrama aimed to put pressure on the representation of the real so as to allow the unrepresented or repressed to achieve material presence' (Starks, 2002, p. 191).

Characterized by the desire to show 'all', the Ramsay films became texts that employed other registers of sign such as non-verbal language, hyperbolic gestures and exaggerated acting styles for heightened affectivity. Consider the opening of a film from the Ramsays' stable, *Bandh Darwaza* that represents the Ramsay approach. There is no build-up to suspense. A pan shot of an old decrepit cavernous ruin cuts quickly to a mid-shot of the slow opening of a coffin from which protrudes a hand followed by a full frontal shot that reveals the monstrous Neola (Anirudh Agarwal) and a voiceover fills in the audience with the monster's repulsive legacy (Figure 5.2). Like a conventional song sequence that disrupts narrative temperance, Neola's introduction in the prefatory sequences of *Bandh Darwaza*, even as the credits roll off, is a standalone single melodramatic sequence that bears out on an 'as is where is' basis, disconnected and disjointed with the sequence that follows immediately. The decontextualized sequence displaces the emphasis of the narrative onto itself way out of proportion.

Extreme close-up shots of the blood-sucking fiend are followed by a medium frontal shot of Neola rising from his

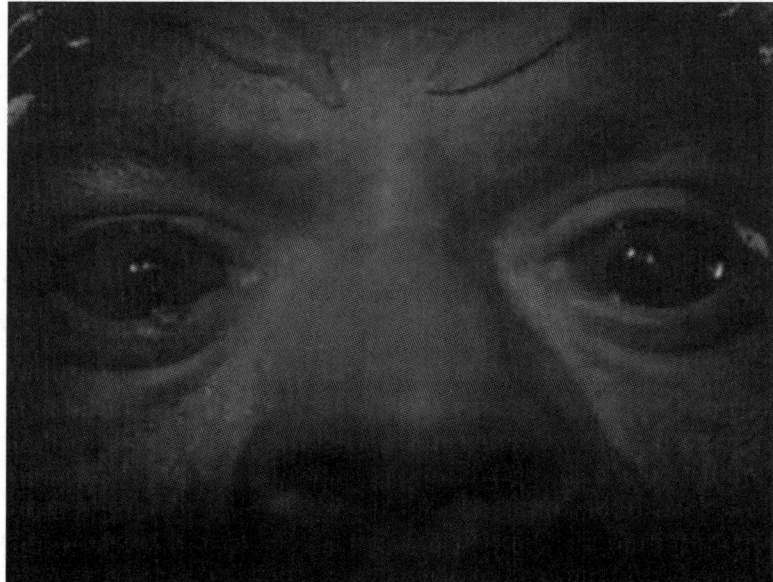

Figure 5.2: A close-up of the monster in the opening shot that reveals all and leaves nothing to the imagination marked the overarching discourse of excess of melodrama in Ramsay Brothers' *Bandh Darwaza*.
Courtesy: Ramsay Productions.

coffin; nothing is left for the imagination. Characters do not stumble upon the monstrous; instead, the narration blazingly opens with the monstrous. The opening sequences of the Ramsays are moments of face-off between the monster and the audience. With monstrosities given blatant introductions early on, the narratives find no urgency to build up on suspense and digress into songs and comic situations. This marks the difference between the horrors of the 1960s with their emphasis on the 'Unseen' to the horror of the 1980s with their prominence to the 'Obvious'.

Contrast this with the bourgeoisie 'aesthetics of subtleties' in *Raat* (Varma, 1992) that marked the post-liberalization entry of mainstream filmmakers where heightened camera mobility and subjective camera shots appropriate the look of the ghost/monster but do not show the ghost/monster itself. The most striking is the opening sequence of *Raat* (Varma, 1992) where Manisha (Revathi) gets off from a bus at a deserted location in broad daylight. Startled by a sight inside an abandoned car Manisha backs away in horror. Yet instead of a reverse shot which would reveal what Manisha sees, the steadicam frustrates the audience's vision by appropriating the 'look' of the spectral presence and hotly pursues her through a lengthy sequence of arrhythmic shots finally trapping her inside a room. As the camera closes in for a 'kill', a cut reveals this to be a nightmare, and the monstrous is withheld from the audience. The ghost who remains invisible makes an appearance within the final minutes of the narrative—refusal to grant full visibility to the ghost/monster becomes a narrative strategy attuned for the post-liberalization middle-class geared cinema. There are attempts to avoid excessive melodramatic representation of blood and gore that we find in the horror films of the Ramsays, and the camera shows reticence in exhibiting horror beyond that which is absolutely necessary. The horror lies not in the monster/ghost's visual—but in its withdrawal. Visual restraint differentiates the spectral presence in the horror films of the 1990s, prolonging the audience's expectation through extended period of absence of the monster/ghost, marking new aesthetics of the Hindi horror genre and swinging the genre away from explicit 'blood and gore' back to the psychological and suggestive elements of horror of the 1960s.

The Ramsay classic monster/ghost demanded full visibility and fetishization but given their budgetary constraints, the mismatch between their cinematic ambitions and visualization was sutured through the cinematic compensation of the aesthetics of melodrama, fantastic monstrous bodies, exaggerated makeup, prosthetic assemblage, primitive visual and acoustic affects, slapstick digressions and grotesque morphology for the putatively less 'aesthetically refined' and more 'direct audiences' in exhibition centres across Indian suburbia. With the introduction of the Video Cassette Recorders (VCRs) and the VHS format that fragmented audiences and weaned away spectators, most of the single theatres that catered to Ramsays' viewership closed down. The easy availability of pornography across different viewing formats meant that sex need not be cloaked within the narratives of the genre of horror. And to counter the Cable TV networks and cheap CDs, producers sought to assuage their losses by selling satellite rights. The Ramsays production house with its repertoire of stock actors, meagre production values and sex content petered out and found few takers. As the number of single theatres dwindled in the 1990s, in the face of cinema reaching drawing rooms through VCRs and the cable TV industry, the sleazy horror genre would have died out had it not been rescued in the CD format, where its competition with mainstream horror was less acute. It resurfaced in films that seemingly straddled horror and soft porn through titles such as *Pyaasi Chudail* (Thirsty Witch) (Rafi, 1998), *Ek Raat Shaitaan Ke Saath* (One Night with Satan) (Malhotra, 1998), *Kunwari Chudail* (Virgin Witch) (Neelam, 2002).

The dissolution of the single theatre systems from around the late 1980s triggered a reduction in the sexual explicitness of horror films. From the mid-1990s, 'the self-representations of the film industry have been marked by a narrative of increasing respectability accruing to the profession' and its need and desire for respectability and acceptance within middle-class ethos (Ganti, 2009, p. 89). The prosthetically enhanced monsters/ghosts in a Ramsay production were a material signifier of the visual excess commensurate with the semi-urban viewership that the Ramsay Brothers served. In contrast, the visually reticent ghost, which made its debut with Ram Gopal Varma's *Raat*, is introduced through highly stylized shaky and imperfect fluid subjective camera movements and is a ghost whose sight is meticulously withheld from the viewers. This was geared for a relatively bourgeoisified middle-class spectatorship, in which the brashness of artificially enhanced monstrosity was traded for middle-class sobriety. In this light, Ram Gopal Varma's oeuvre should be seen as the result of cultural shifts engendered by political and economic changes rather than aesthetic revisions driven by a single *auteur*. Through this seemingly deliberate break with previous visual style and cinematic aesthetic the horror genre was gearing itself once again for middle-class respectability.

Economic reforms unfettered the Indian markets and luxurious consumption that carried the stigma of Western materialism was delinked from opulence and decadence. Through alignment with advanced global capital, Indian audiences' preferences for classy romantic comedies and action films put pressure on the B-grade Hindi horror filmmakers, squeezing them out of the market. With easier access to English horror films which offered better production values, and the simultaneous introduction of CDs in India, the Hindi horror films of the Ramsay and the Bhakri Brothers eventually gave way. Another reason for the decline of horror filmmakers like Ramsay Brothers (producers of

Bandh Darwaza), who like the Hammer Productions house had produced myriad range of films in the horror genre, was the taking over of the horror genre by mainstream Hindi filmmakers who brought the level of sex and sleaze to negligible levels, thereby attracting the family audiences and expanding beyond their niche audience.

This brings us to the subgenre fashioned in the Post-Hindutva milieu. Both the traditional–cultural narrative and the Hindutva ideological seek to radically critique the underpinnings of the non-sectarian Indian State and pursue a reassessment of post-colonial Indian identity. But in what ways does the Hindutva ideological subgenre appropriate and unconsciously recycle and represent a collective projection of majoritarian fantasies? To understand the promulgated meanings one must comprehend the way in which films have interacted with and resonated within larger social constellations.

From the 1980s onwards, 'Hindu nationalist parties especially the electorally successful were able to win millions of votes—by claiming that groups outside the Hindu 'family' especially Muslims and Christians—benefitted disproportionately from the post-colonial states' secular policies' (Haynes, 1999, p. 14). The late 1980s saw the rise of overt Hindu confessional politics amid the general decline of Centrist politics which envisioned, at least theoretically, a neutral role for the state. 'Aided by the proliferation of religious symbolism in the print and the electronic media, Hindu themes and organizations crossed state boundaries and helped diverse sects, castes and classes to acquire consciousness of a popular and more homogeneous Hinduism' (Rudolph & Rudolph, 1987, p. 41). The decade of the 1980s saw the broadcast of mythological TV serials like Ramayana (Sagar, 1987) and Mahabharata (Chopra, 1990) whose cultural imports allowed for the resurrection and revival of latent *Hindutva* consciousness which could later be politicized into cultural nationalism.

In certain cases watching the weekly [TV] episodes [of the mythological epics] was considered an act of devotion ... its success led
in turn to all activities being suspended on Sunday mornings when
the broadcast was taking place—the average audience was estimated at 91% of those owning a TV set. (Jaffrelot, 1996, p. 389)

As Victoria Farmer points out, 'these serials, on the whole
'projected an India that was overwhelmingly north Indian,
Hindi speaking, middle class, and Hindu' (Farmer, 2000,
p. 267). Vaishnavism and the worship of Lord Rama, a competing current of Hinduism within the larger family of con-
tending Hinduism philosophies prevalent mostly in North
India, sought to displace a diversity of Hindu Gods, and
accord Hinduism with attributes of Semitic religions.

By 1991 India had no foreign reserve to pay for its imports.
Deficit spending led to inflation and declining exports
threatened to further deplete scarce foreign reserves. Bad
planning and not socialist rhetoric brought Indian economy
on the verge of economic meltdown. To improve fiscal fit-
ness and reorient the public sector units away from their
sluggishness, competition was introduced and monopolis-
tic tendencies were curbed. Foreign investors wanting to do
business in India, which boasted of a sizeable middle class
brought in the much-needed capital that could offset the
balance of payment crisis.

This opening up of the Indian economy directly influenced the media industry. With the open skies policy in
place, Indian satellite television was pitted in direct competition with cinema in terms of spectatorship. The Gulf War
and its live broadcast to affluent Indian homes heralded the
satellite TV age. Its ease of intrusion into Indian drawing
rooms was first decried as an invasion of the cultural kind.
This anti-invasion brigade predicated itself on the 'rhetoric of cultural nationalism, which called for the protection
of Indian airwaves, and thus Indian culture, from foreign
broadcast' (Farmer, 2000, p. 274). By 1999, about 900 million people in India had access to a TV set, and television

audience which was 1.7 million in 1973 reached 500 million. In the same year there were about 65 million TV sets in India (Singhal & Rogers, 2001, p. 87). Doordarshan lost its monopoly over entertainment to broadcast from abroad.

Reforms and the opening of the Indian skies brought Western lifestyle directly into Indian drawing rooms fed on a diet of state-sponsored broadcasts on Doordarshan. This ushered in consolidation of middle-class conspicuous consumption and delinked Western materialism from wealth. But this period was also marked by an onset of a full blown out Pakistan supported insurgency in Kashmir that despite claiming sub-nationalist origins was increasingly defining itself in Islamist terms. A reciprocal vitalization of political Hinduism through the politics of Hindutva and the general acceptance of a particularistic view of Indian nationhood that could only be realized through the ideals of cultural nationalism espoused by reinvigorated rightwing political parties called for a renegotiation of the frameworks of Indian secularism.

In these trying circumstances 'the film industry itself insecure with the advent and growing popularity of satellite television responded wholeheartedly to the definition of 'Indian' culture offered by proponents of Hindutva' (Vishwanath, 2002, p. 41). The action thriller underwent profound transformations that went well beyond mere improvisation of pyrotechnics. The ambiguity of the external enemy gave way to open identification of Pakistan as mortal existential threat. Wealth and consumption were reconfigured into the Non-resident Indian (NRI) narratives of the 1990s. The opening of the diasporic markets and the growing influence made it imperative to tap into the affluent markets that looked upon Hindi cinema as a means of realignment with the home left behind. The 1990s marked the de-territorialization of Hindi cinema. Mode of consumption shaped modes of expression. The steady decline of the single theatres with larger seating capacities and lower-price tickets gave way to multiplex audiences with much smaller seating capacities and higher-price tags. These multiplexes exhibiting their wares could focus on offbeat themes and still remain economically viable. The Ramsay Brothers, with their abandoned *havelis* (mansions) and secular ghosts equally 'susceptible' to other faiths, were seen as 'unwelcome[d] intruders in the movie industry's onward march to bourgeoisie respectability' (Nair, 2009) and were eased out of the horror genre by mainstream Hindi film-makers. They expanded the genre beyond its niche small town audiences, and pitched the horror genre to the emerging Indian middle class that was increasingly receptive to *Hindutva's* rhetoric of cultural nationalism.

The previous decade had seen contests around caste identities which culminated in reservations for lower caste Hindus which was looked upon by the middle class, upper caste Hindus as another fragmentation of the nation and a direct threat to their entrenched hegemonic position within the state apparatus. This manifested their eventual shift to majoritarian politics. By the early 1990s, the apparent failures of self-avowed secular polity engendered a belief that the Indian State could be held together only by its Hindu majority bound together by a monolithic Hinduism manifesting itself through *Hindutva*. The *Hindutva* oriented cultural nationalism was marked by attempts at 'construction of histories or lineages as morale boosters, for legitimacy to link up present aspiration with more or less imagined pasts in efforts to move towards specific kinds of future' (Sarkar, 2002, p. 246). *Hindutva* historiography presented the medieval imperial struggle between the Rajputs and the Mughals as Hindu–Muslim existential battles and medieval history as the dark ages 'marked by Muslim invasions and conquests, obliteration of Hindu ancient glory, forced conversions, and the destruction of temples' (Sarkar, 2002, p. 247). In 1995, the Indian Supreme Court declared 'Hindutva wasn't religion but a way of life, to be understood as a synonym of "indianization," i.e., development of uniform culture by obliterating the differences between all the cultures coexisting in the country'(Noorani, 2006, p. 77). But as Richard H. Davis points out 'Hindutva' literally means Hindu-ness and has become ... widely accepted as shorthand for referring to various groups and projects that aim at redefining India as a Hindu *Rashtra* or Hindu nation' (Davis, 2005, p. 109). The narration of *1920* marks an emerging subgenre within the Hindi horror cinema, in its infancy as yet, where evil is disinclined towards, and indignant about the therapeutic and prophylactic values offered by the faith of religious minorities in India, being reflective of subtle changes taking place off-screen. It is in this context that *1920's* ideological project must be unmasked.

1920

Towards the climax of Vikram Bhatt's horror film *1920* (Bhatt, 2008), the narration reveals its ideological mooring as a tracking camera brings into frame a possessed Liza (Adah Sharma) lying on a bed even as Father Thomas (Raj Zutshi) begins to recite 'Our Father in Heaven'. The Lord's Prayer has significant therapeutic value in Christian theology, being the only prayer attributed to Jesus Christ in the New Testament. It appears twice: first in Matthew 6: 9-13 as part of the *Sermon on the Mount*: 'In this manner, therefore, pray: Our Father in Heaven'. And the second time in Luke 11: 2-4: 'So He said to them, "when you pray, say: Our Father in Heaven, hallowed be Your name"'. Father Thomas begins the recitation:

> In the name of the Father, and the Son, and the Holy Spirit, I cast you out unclean spirit along with every spectre from Hell, and all your fallen companion in the name of the our Lord Jesus Christ. Be gone; and stay away far from this creature of God. For it is He who commands you; He who flung you headlong from the heights of Heaven to the depths of Hell. (Bhatt, 2008)

In *1920* (Bhatt, 2008), this Christian exorcism utterly fails to dislodge the evil spirit, eliciting a taunting reaction but nothing much beyond that, signifying the (im)potency of Christian practice. Predictably Father Thomas is killed, while the unfinished exorcism is brought to a successful conclusion not through the *Lord's Prayer* but by the recitation of *Hanuman Chalisa*[1] by Arjun Singh Rathore.

Concurrently, the disjunction between tradition and modernity created by *Jadu Tona*, but cleverly papered over in its narrative closure, breaks down in *1920* (Bhatt, 2008) which abandons the cultural inclusivity of *Jadu Tona*, reverses the subordination of the spiritual to the secular order and introduces a new Hindutva discourse in the Hindi horror genre. Reflective of Hindutva's discourse, *1920* is a post-Hindutva Hindi horror film, released in an unsettling irony, close to anti-Christian violence in Kandhamal in the eastern Indian province of Orissa in 2008 and is emblematic of its newly emergent subgenre. The Hindutva ideologic orientation of *1920* explicitly introduces a three-way contest between traditional Hindu spirituality, scientific rationalism and Christianity. The plot revolves around a case of possession and creates a narrative space that brings about overlapping and competing claims between Hindu traditionalism, Christian theology and the secular–scientific rational thought. The benign folk traditionalism of *Jadu Tona* redefines itself purely in Hindutva terms in *1920*.

A critical examination of the visual strategies brought into the narrative will, I hope, provide perceptivities into the larger representational politics at work. While maintaining spatial aloofness from contemporaneous Indian events *1920* nevertheless concerns itself with the anxieties of a Hindu-nationalist discourse and is about Arjun Singh, a Hindu, and his Christian wife Liza who, in course of the narration, is possessed by an evil spirit. If Ameer Chand's contemptuous rejection of the traditional and the tralatitious marked the opening of *Jadu Tona*, the introductory sequence of *1920* is a yearning for a reintroduction of the sacred into the 'quotidian'. As an architect who might possibly be western educated, Arjun Singh's credentials of a tradition-honouring Hindu are firmly demonstrated where he is introduced through a tracking shot, engrossed in his early morning traditional Hindu rituals. Recalling the representational conventions employed by foreign travellers, amateur photographers and imperial documentary filmmakers, the opening of *1920* draws on common ethnographic conventions of framing the 'native' in his mundane living space, re-enacting his cultural specificities for an ethnographic gaze. Extreme close-ups of his bare-bodied performance of ablutionary rituals in just loin cloth fetishize his Hindu identity in the opening shot, and the hero is framed within the iconicity of his community. In one frame, Arjun returning from his walk is placed in the extreme right with a cow centre spaced in the frame (Figure 5.3).

His caste-breaching love affair with Liza, born out of an illicit relationship between a Hindu woman and an Englishman, burnishes his liberal credentials. Fearing that his love match would not be accepted by his staunchly

Figure 5.3: A cow is centre-spaced in the frame as Arjun returns from his walk. *Courtesy:* ASA Production & Enterprises.

traditional father, the couple attempt escape but their car is waylaid and following a brief fight sequence, the father harangues him for falling for a 'half-caste' Liza. Equally incensed in turn, Arjun denounces the Hindu *sanskar*[2] yanks off his *janyu*, the sacred thread worn by upper caste Hindu men, and symbolically renounces his Hindu faith.

Yet the 'secular' order established through this act of renunciation is informed and triggered by Arjun's desire to seek vengeance on his father and not latent agnostic thought. It is transient, imposed and this dissonance between Arjun's traditional past and his 'atheist secular' present will be resolved later. The couple move into a mansion, where unknown to them an evil spirit awaits to carry out its long-term project of revenge, and Liza's conjugality is disrupted by strange voices at night. Later, as Liza seeks out a church, the Christian theological claim is introduced through two prefatorial shots that bring in the church and the priest into the film's narrative and symbolically present the faith's unsophistication, marking the everydayness and vulnerability of its earthly manifestations. Liza's gaze appropriated through a subjective high-angle camera shot which implicates the viewer into the narrative, presents the Church's cross hanging unsteadily from the spire (Figure 5.4).

Father Thomas (Raj Zutshi) is shown engaged in another temporal activity: raking dry leaves in the church's compound. At the connotative level, Father Thomas' fair skin and auburn hair denotes the foreignness of Christian missionaries. At the mythical level, it entraps meaning within the *alleged* foreignness of Father Thomas, asserting the faith is foreign. The subtext of 'forced' proselytization[3] becomes apparent when the priest expresses wonder at Liza's surname and yet *expects* Liza to bring her Hindu husband at the next Sunday Mass.

Father Thomas implicates the Christian faith into the emerging contest and initiates the first skirmish with evil by sprinkling holy water in the mansion's haunted room. Peril

Figure 5.4: The precariously perched cross atop the church introduces the faith and its ordinariness in *1920*.
Courtesy: ASA Production & Enterprises.

is deferred, albeit temporarily, and the priest's misplaced optimism heightens his and his God's humiliation. Far from being expelled, the evil spirit rattles the priest in his own Presbytery, proclaiming that its overarching transgressive reach and its power can extend beyond its haunt, and onto the realm of the holy but ineffective church. Unlike the subtly effective numerical 786 in *Jadu Tona*, which marked cultural inclusivity and established Islamic potency in deterring evil, the sprinkling of the holy water in *1920* is devoid of any therapeutic value and utterly fails. Undeterred, the spirit visits Liza and finally possesses her. Without the safety net of cultural constructs to sort out the abject from the object, the boundary between the two collapses and Liza becomes a cultural abomination as she relishes a dead cat. And it is here that the monstrous difference becomes almost a cultural taboo — while flesh eating itself is not anti-cultural it is located with the normative parameters organized by the discourse of majoritarianism and produces revulsion for being 'unclean' and 'polluted'.

With a narrative crisis thus precipitated a possessed Liza becomes a contested territory between the scientific–secular thought as signified by the doctor (Shri Vallabh Vyas) brought in to 'cure' Liza; the Christian theological perspective personified by Father Thomas who 'believes' Liza to be possessed and the ideologic–dogmatic as signified by Arjun Singh Rathore who will, post dissonance, return to his Hindu faith. While Father Thomas requests an exorcism, the doctor swears by 'personality disorder' as he invokes a certain Doctor Freud's work in Vienna on split personality. But the secular–rational thought which had a put a brave front through Dr Vikram in *Jadu Tona* is declared 'base and immoral' in *1920*. A possessed Liza reveals lurid sexual details from the doctor's seedy past forcing him to abandon her. Scientific–secularism 'discredited and dishonoured' accepts defeat and recedes into oblivion.

The failure of the secular marks the beginning of a dyad contest between the two remaining contestants. An atheist Arjun remembering Liza's faith in her God seeks Father Thomas to 'heal' her. The second recovery attempt through a recital of the Lord's Prayer is mocked at by the spirit which levitates Liza in a mock Christ-like pose with her arms outstretched in a derisive show of crucifixion and promises to kill her on *amavasya* (the moonless night). By contesting and reacting to the Father's spiritual device, the evil spirit 'concedes' the Christian God's benign yet harmless presence, but refuses to yield 'space' to Him. Former caretaker reveals the evil spirit to be that of Mohan Kant (Indraneil Sengupta), a collaborator in the revolt of 1857, mistakenly given refuge in the mansion by Gayatri Devi (Anjolie Alagh), who later in an act of atonement entraps him. The old female caretaker infers that Liza is Gayatri Devi's reincarnation.

The veritable subtextuality of 'the anti-national' as a source of anxiety in the post-Hindutva age manifests in the identification of evil spirit with that of a collaborator. Liza's interposition now as a reincarnation of Gayatri Devi, finds favour with the priest from a faith that does not subscribe to reincarnation. While Christian dogma speaks of resurrection, there is no scriptural basis for rebirth in Christianity. With this thesis of reincarnation receiving all-round acceptance even from those who would at least theoretically be required to contest it, the narrative's stance is explicitly outlined and invites uninterrupted audience's identification.

1920's discourse thus assigns a hegemonic role for Hinduism, and legitimizes its encroaching role. The last and final attempt at exorcism is conducted by Father Thomas again. But with a ghost who has already made known where his strengths and vulnerabilities lie, any application of exorcist ritual not emerging from Hindu rituals is reduced to a debilitating embarrassing 'farce'. The final skirmish between Father Thomas and the evil spirit, becomes a game of 'creative intimidation' in which the priest 'sees' his holy stole turns into a slithering serpent. As a horrified Father Thomas throws away his stole, he is mocked at by the evil spirit: *The fear of the serpent made you abandon God. Now What?* Christian theology presents the snake as a symbol of temptation. Satan appears as a serpent before Adam and Eve to tempt them with the Original Sin. The commission of the Original Sin puts Adam beyond reconciliation with God and leads to his disgrace. The priest likewise succumbs to the 'temptation' of imagining his stole as a serpent and becomes a fallen man beyond the mercy and redemption of his God. Father Thomas is dragged inside the haunted room and impaled by an iron poker. His strategically placed death renounces his claim on spiritual proficiency and becomes a spurious attempt at his valourization. The Christian God, extant but unable to influence events now, fails to protect Father Thomas because of the wavering faith. Father Thomas' (un)ceremonious exit brings an end to this diarchic power play and re-contextualizes the exclusivist narrative within the overarching discourse of majoritarianism. The engagement is thus monopolized by a discourse from which all competing claimants have been purged. With the Christian theology thus neutralized, the evil spirit flings Arjun away and challenges him to save Liza's life. An extreme close-up shot of Arjun Singh lying injured on the floor is followed by a series of cutaway shots of an idol of Lord Hanuman, implying *darshan* (seeing the divine) (Figure 5.5).

As Melanie Wright writes, '*Darshan* [is] experiencing the presence of the divine through the act of seeing an image of a God or a saint—[and] is an important form of Hindu worship' (Wright, 2007, p. 151). Accompanied by the non-diegetic sound of conch-shell blowing, which marks his final reconciliation with, and return to the Hindu order, Arjun Singh Rathore recites the *Hanuman Chalisa*. In Hindu mythology, the blowing of the conch shell heralds the victory of good over evil and is used to initiate religious ceremonies. Lord Vishnu, the God of preservation, is portrayed holding a conch in his hand. The exorcism becomes a ceremony with ternary functions: a Christian rediscovers her Hindu roots, a Hindu recovers his lost faith, and an anti-national force is

Figure 5.5: The cutaway shot of the Hindu God Hanuman implying *darshan* for Arjun Singh Rathore in *1920*.
Courtesy: ASA Production & Enterprises.

exorcised. The evil spirit finally abandons Liza's body and explodes in a conclusive show of defeat.

Arjun Singh Rathore's character parallels that of the warrior prince Arjun of the Hindu epic Mahabharata who suffers a 'crisis of faith', turns pacifist and refuses to go to war with his cousins, the *Kauravas*. It is only on Lord Krishna's polemic in favour of *Dharma* or duty without expectation of rewards or consequences that turn Arjun around and make him wage war against his kinsmen. Metaphorically, Liza's possession becomes an act through which Arjun Singh overcomes the spiritual agnosticism and reconciles with his lost Hindu faith, much like the possession of Harsha in *Jadu Tona* which triggers Varsha's reconciliation with the traditional.

The two divergent thought streams manifesting through Baba Bajrangi and the secular–rationalist Dr Kailash of *Jadu Tona* is merged together in Arjun Singh. Once this is affected, modernity becomes the means of sustaining tradition for the new social order. The successiveness of faith, lack of faith and an eventual return to faith, therefore, is like a second birth for Arjun Singh Rathore, who through this act of recovery, becomes twice born and regains his upper-caste identity. His return to the Hindu way of life signifies his *shuddhikaran*, a ritual purification practice used by Hindu groups in India to convert non-Hindus into Hindus. Arjun's physical attributes: tall height, wide chest and broad shoulders, coupled with his fearlessness, symbolize an assertive Hindu virility. Arjun's God becomes merciful, all embracing, overarching, dominant, ever forgiving, and non-exacting unlike the God of Father Thomas. Finally, the spirit itself shows where its allegiance lies, for it is through its machinations that the play of opportunities is set in motion where Father Thomas and his faith stand totally disgraced and discredited. The evil in *1920* allows Arjun to recover his Hindu faith and assert his spiritual superiority. The Hindutva ideologic lays exclusive claim over the possessed.

Liza's character, with her white skin and dark hairs as an admixture of two races denotes the Anglo-Indian community, which as right-wing Hindu groups often claim, is a convert from Hinduism and must re-adopt Hindu practices. Salvation and deliverance from evil comes to Liza not from her unerring faith in Christ but through Lord Hanuman, whose *darshan* is made available to Arjun. The discourse of *1920* hints that the domain of Hinduism extends far beyond its own spiritual realm. By according some therapeutic values, not all, since the Christian faith remains ineffective against evil, a process of neutralization is affected whereby the faith is stripped of all its oppositional elements (potency to 'cure', spiritual proficiency) endowed with reincarnation and rebirth and subsumed into the Hindu order. *1920*, therefore, privileges a Hindu-centric value at the cost of other competing interests by refusing to entertain other faith's claim on Liza. Meaning encoded in the textual organization of *1920* delivers it to the mechanics of ideology, myth-making and Hindutva polemics. The film maintains an intimate functional relationship with contemporaneous Indian politics, despite its alleged spatial dislocation. The deconstruction of *1920* reveals the power equation between the different 'systems of belief' and unwraps the way it accords a privileged role to 'a way of life'. The periphery of *Madhumati* gravitates towards the centre, and the 'appropriator' of *Madhumati* becomes the 'appropriated' in *1920*.

While earlier films saw exorcism being performed by minor characters incidental to be plot and introduced or reintroduced only in the denouement, *1920* flings the main protagonist into the thick of exorcising activities, making him the initiator rather than an accomplice to the ritual of exorcism. The development of Arjun's character parallels Hinduism's encounter with legal–rationalist Western thought during the Colonial era: disdain for scientific rational thought in the beginning, fascination with scientific–rational discourse, and then finally disenchantment with scientific rationalism in favour of a reformed egalitarian Hinduism, as propagated by Hindu reformers. Enamoured by the rationalist–secular thoughts introduced through the colonial schools and colleges early Hindu pioneers of reforms in the eighteenth century questioned the very basis of Hindu sociopolitical thought, renounced their faiths, and some even converted to Christianity. But these flirtations with Christianity were brief and always remained on the fringes. Traditionalists asserted themselves more forcefully in the post-1857 period and could enjoy a greater degree of autonomy in the traditional sphere. Arjun Singh Rathore starts as a committed traditional Hindu, rejects Hinduism briefly in a fit of rage, but finally reconciles with the Hindu faith.

Haunted

While charting a new cartography of cinematic terrain where the faith of a minority group occupies the centre stage, *Haunted* (Bhatt, 2011) nevertheless shares systematic complicities with the narrative strategies of *1920* and like the post-liberalization monstrous other feminine narratives presents an updated and more responsive Hindutva polemic aware of accusation of self-aggrandizement and thus amenable to hegemonic concerns.

Haunted presents Iyer's decimation/annihilation as the zone of competing interests. The film ostensibly appears to abandon the homogenizing disposition of strident Hindutva and appears accommodative of other faiths, but justly so, presenting a revisionist and a refurbished Hindutva freed from the charges of being a meta-narrative that forcefully subsumes all counter-narratives. Released in 2011, *Haunted* does not explicitly create 'zones of contestations', between competing faiths, and its polemics of hegemony come along less rigorous than the narrative approach of *1920*. *Haunted* is about Rehan (Mahaakshay) representing a real-estate brokerage company and who comes to Koti to sell off the palatial Glen Manor, an estate, and is accosted on the way by a vagrant who says 'only you can do it'. On arrival at the mansion, he is intrigued to find that the caretaker has died under mysterious circumstances, and the other attendants refuse caretaking jobs citing the house to be haunted by an evil spirit. At night Rehan hears screams, inexplicable movements and apparitions within the mansion's precincts. Mrs Stephens (Prachi Shah), a medium brought in to heal the house, warns of a malevolent force and leaves, advising Rehan to depart as well.

Amid recurring paranormal episodes, Rehan chances upon a suicide note purportedly written decades ago by Meera (Tia Bajpai) for her parents in which she details her music teacher Professor Iyer's (Arif Zakaria) bid at molestation in their absence, his accidental death at her hands, his return from the dead, his repeated sexual violations of Meera within Glen Manor, and finally Meera's suicide as an act of escape. Her soul remains trapped within the precincts of Glen Manor where Professor Iyer's evil spirit repeatedly re-enacts the ritual of rape every night.

The mysterious vagrant reappears at Glen Manor and sends Rehan back in time to prevent Meera's attempted rape and Iyer's accidental death that turns him into a vicious vengeance-seeking ghost. Yet despite time travel, Rehan is unable to influence the course of events. Professor Iyer attempts the rape and in the ensuing melee is struck by Meera and dies. Aware now that Iyer's evil soul will return to seek vengeance Rehan convinces Meera about his travel through time and the need to move to a safer location.

Through Meera's Christian maid Margaret (Achint Kaur), Rehan seeks the help of a Christian priest (Mohan Kapoor) and recourse to one faith leads to another. Though the Christian priest shows knowledge of evil spirits, including his 'pearl of wisdom' that spirits become very powerful near the break of dawn and are at their weakest in the afternoon, he appears helpless in confronting evil and instead guides the asylum seekers to a purportedly safer location: the *dargah* of a Sufi saint some miles away, much safer than the precincts of his own hallowed realm, the local church. Unlike Father Thomas in *1920* the priest in *Haunted* makes no pretences about his or his faith's potencies and instead relegates himself merely to praying for their safe journey. Yet, in a manner reminiscent of 1920, the Christian priest is bitten by a snake and dies ignominiously.

On their way to the *dargah*, the entourage seeks refuge in a hotel at night, where Margaret, the housemaid, is possessed and in an act loaded with blatant lesbian connotations tries to rape Meera. Rehan drives a cross into Margaret's back that provides them with temporary reprieve and a momentary head start in a final rush to the *dargah*. The cross with its limited therapeutic value is able to stave off Prof. Iyer's soul only temporarily.

With a possessed Margaret in hot pursuit, the couple manages to reach the *dargah* and in the subsequent struggle Rehan drags Margaret inside the *dargah*, who is immediately repulsed by the saint's divinity. The tramp who accosted Rehan in the beginning of the narration is revealed to be the *dargah's* Sufi. With verses from the Koran decorating the walls of his *dargah*, the Sufi appears potent in repelling evil, but like the Christian priest before him, refrains from confronting Iyer's spirit reasoning, 'God gave me powers to see beyond but not the permission to intervene. The Sufi reveals that Meera can be 'untied' from Iyer's evil spirit only when *paanchtattva* (the five elements) composed of fire, water, air, earth, and *rooh* (spirit) are dropped in a well, supposedly blessed by Khwaja Khizr. The Sufi elaborates that God, the Almighty, created the heaven, the earth and everything in between with five elements. The sympathetic Sufi expresses inability to intervene in earthly matters, but can, quite paradoxically, teleport Rehan back to the past to change the course of the present. Rehan undertakes the final journey to the blessed well with Meera, where after a ferocious struggle with Iyer, Meera's pendant stained with Iyer's blood is put out in the blessed well. Iyer's evil soul is vanquished, but Rehan too slips in the well and reaches back in the present. The letter kept for him in a book reveals that Meera married and went on to live to a ripe old age.

The Hindu scripture *Svetasvatara Upanishad* in its Chapter 6 Verse 2 says:

> He by whom the whole universe is constantly pervaded is the Knower, the Author of time. He is sinless and omniscient. It is at His command that the work which is called earth, water, fire, air and akasa appears as the universe. All this should be reflected upon by the wise. (Svetasvatara Upanishad)

Again the *Taittiriya Upanishad* speaks:

> So from this Atman has sprung Ether and from Ether, Air; from Air, Fire; from Fire, Water; from Water, Earth; from Earth vegetables; from vegetables, food; from food man. (Sharyananda, 1921, p. 53).

Hindu scriptural texts such as *Chandogya Upanishad* and the *Taittiriya Upanishad* describe the genesis of the five elements. Rene Guenon writes, 'each element corresponds a sensible quality ... by which the latter [element] is known to us ... to ether corresponds hearing (*shrotra*); to air, touch (*vach*); to fire, sight (*chakshus*); to water, taste (*vasana*); and to earth, smell (*ghrana*)' (Guenon, 2004, p. 31). According to the Hindu view, 'the physical body is based to have been produced out of the five elements of earth, water, light, wind, and ether' (Morgan, 1987, p. 123). Death can affect only the physical body and nothing else and at the death of the individual only the physical body perishes and dissolves into the five elements out of which it is produced. Symbolically, Iyer's body is to be reconstituted before its destruction into baser elements. The assembling of the five elements by Rehan becomes a quasi-funeral proceeding without which Iyer's soul cannot leave the realm of the living.

While the Koran speaks of Djinns being created from fire (Ch. 15, V: 27) and Adam being created from 'mud' (Ch. 7, V: 12), it does not subscribe to the five elements philosophy. The narration subtly introduces the Hindu philosophical subtext within the larger Muslim spiritual discourse of *Sufism*. Like Father Thomas in *1920*, the Muslim saint can rebuff but not annihilate evil which can materialize only when the five elements of creation assemble and Iyer's blood stains are doused in the water of the sacred well. So when the Sufi demands that Iyer's ghost be annihilated through recourse to the *paanchtattva*, he essentially satisfies the long-held demand of the Hindu right for an autochthonic Islam that is sufficiently grounded in local sensibilities to merit acceptance. The shift from the Christian priest to the Muslim fakir-saint presented not as a wielder of Islamic identity within the narrative but as a signifier to a larger truth — the truth of the *paanchtattvas* is a crucial moment, for it is here that the fakir Muslim saint stands deified exalted and morphed into an idealized spirit or *atma* transcending time and space.

In this context, it is important to recall the ideological continuities between *1920* and *Haunted*. If *1920* presented Liza's body as the realm of contest, *Haunted* presents Iyer's evil soul as the zone of competition, whose annihilation engineers a friendly competition between faiths. The *peer* is potent enough to repel evil but justly so, leaving the final confrontation with evil to Rehan's tryst with the *panchtattvas* or five elements. Recourse to the *peer* Muslim saint materializes only when the Church through its protagonist, the unnamed priest seeks an early exit from the narrative, and reiterates its own (spiritual) incapacity to confront evil. If Father Thomas had brought on a head-on clash with malefic forces in *1920*, *Haunted*'s Christian priest meekly surrenders all claims to spiritual benignancy and instead asks Rehan to seek refuge elsewhere. As an empty sign devoid of all significations the priest in *Haunted* is reduced to pointing out direction to other equally less potent signs.

The dominant structural trait of *Haunted* appears to be sign constructions where each rival claimant merely withdraws from the contest after pointing the way out to another sign. The Christian priest expresses his inability to help the couple and instead directs them to the tomb of a Muslim saint restricting himself to praying for their safe journey. The anonymous Muslim *peer* of the *dargah* owns up to his inability either to intervene or restrain Professor Iyer's evil spirit. The mysterious well supposedly blessed by the mystical Khwaja Khizr will send Iyer's soul to hell but not before all the *paanchtattvas* (five elements) have been assembled and are doused in its hallowed water. Each insignificant article of faith points to another inconsequential article of faith in turn becoming an empty signifier, organizing the contradictions in the diegetic world of *Haunted*. It is in this way that *Haunted* becomes a refurbished *1920*. The climax of *1920* and *Haunted* close down all alternative meanings and figurations. In their resolutions the Hindu exorcism eliminates all other potential alternatives, ideological threats, competing value systems and reinforces the status quo. But since the dominant ideology is inherently unstable as it faces newer resistance constantly which can be only overcome but never truly eliminated, it must constantly rework towards newer forms of domination. All forms of resistance are worked into the dominant ideology to deny them their oppositionality.

Conclusion

Thus, an exploration of the cinematic subjectivities of the genre reveals that each specific historical moment has affected the Hindi horror genre which, in turn, through its spectral beings and their eventual decimation has allowed interplay between competing worldviews, affording them to idealize and valourize themselves in the bargain.

A reiteration is necessary here. The Hindi horror genre with its common traits of narrative engagements, aesthetic stratagems and iconographic representations bears the unity of a genre which is marked by shifting plays of narrations that continuously imagines and reimages the nation in terms of dominant forms of discourse. Like the nation, the genre is perpetually under construction, a work in progress. Prior to its engagement with the horror genre the first chapter posits that right through its inception and originary moment, Hindi cinema has been firmly imbricated in projecting nationalist goals. The second chapter lays bare the larger debates pertaining to formulations of the genre per se and the place of the *auteur* within it, progressing to inform the various positions and elucidates upon the generic qualities of the Hindi horror cinema, its convergences with a range of extra-national cinematic movements, and its unique departures in terms of its ideological concerns and distinctive generic contours. The third chapter posits that a small body of horror films beginning with *Mahal* and later substantiated by *Madhumati* laid the foundations of the genre; its narrative schemes reflecting idealized Nehruvian secularism. The fourth chapter argues that beginning with post-Emergency, a number of horror films marked their narratives with stark disillusionment with the discourse of secularism and scientific–rationalism even as they sought to deify the discourse of traditional–culturalism and deployed suitably reinvigorated and inclusivist Hindu folklore derived myths to aesthetically and cinematically challenge the demands of scientific rationalism. The final chapter argues that consonant with and being reflective of larger social forces at work, the broad consensus on the *Carnivalesque* moments in the traditional–cultural narratives has given way to an overtly Hindu subaltern religiosity from which all rival claims have been suitably purged and stripped of their therapeutics, marking a tectonic shift which is visible across other genres. Perceptibly, Hindi horror films are being released even as I write and measuring a period becomes difficult if we are still immersed in it. The Hindutva ideologic subgenre as I have noted in the book is in its infancy as yet. However, Hindi horror cinema in its contemporary drive, for at least some time to come, will meander through varied aesthetic and thematic drives towards consensual hegemony and ideological conformity in which all narratives will lead to the same goalpost: narratives in which the 'Other' will be subsumed into the order of the Self. Hindi horror genre is, therefore, not just responding to the call of business only, but through newer generic infusions and varying permutations of the horror codes is profoundly a site of reactions to sociohistorical changes.

Notes

1. Hindu devotional poem was written by Tulsi Das (1532–1623 AD) in praise of Lord Hanuman, the monkey God and a devotee of Lord Rama in the epic Ramayana. The recitation of Hanuman Chalisa is said to have therapeutic value against evil spirits.
2. Upadhyay and Pandey mention that *sanskar* is 'the satisfaction of total Hindu rituals' (Upadhyay & Pandey, 1993). There are 16 important *sanskars* — the important ones being birth, *mundan* or the ritual of shaving of the hair of a newborn; *janyu*, the sacred thread worn over the right shoulder by upper-caste men and its accompanying ceremony; etc. Through the performance of these *sanskars* a man becomes a social being.
3. States of Gujarat, Tamil Nadu, Madhya Pradesh, Orissa and Arunachal Pradesh have passed various laws that require intimation of religious conversion to government officials. In some Indian states, religious conversion requires the newly converted to produce a legal affidavit that he/she was not under any pressure, force or allurement to convert but was converting by own will and desire.

References

Abbas, K. A. (Director). (1969). *Saat hindustani* [Motion Picture]. India: Naya Sansar.

Akbar, A. (Director). (2007). *Gauri: The unborn* [Motion Picture]. India: AD Labs & Myth Productions.

Alam, J. (1999). *India: Living with modernity*. New Delhi: Oxford University Press.

Allen, L. (Director). (1944). *The uninvited* [Motion Picture]. USA: Paramount Pictures.

————. (Director). (1945). *The unseen* [Motion Picture]. USA: Paramount Pictures.

Altman, R. (1997). Cinema and genre. In G. Nowell-Smith (Ed.), *The Oxford history of world cinema* (pp. 276–285). London: Oxford university Press.

Amrohi, K. (Director). (1949). *Mahal* [Motion Picture]. India: Bombay Talkies.

Anand, C. (Director). (1964). *Haqeeqat* [Motion Picture]. India: Himalaya Films.

————. (Director). (1973). *Hindustan ki kasam* [Motion Picture]. India: Sneh Films.

Anand, S., & Chibber, S. R. (Directors). (2013). *3G* [Motion Picture]. India: Eros Entertainment & Next Gen Films.

Anderson, P. W. (Director). (2002). *Resident evil* [Motion Picture]. USA: Sony Pictures.

Andrew, D. (1993). The unauthorized autuer today. In J. Collins, H. Radner & A. P. Collins (Eds), *Film theory goes to the movies* (pp. 77–85). New York: Routledge.

Ansari, N. A. (Director). (1962). *Tower house* [Motion Picture]. India: Desh Productions.

Arnold, D. (1999). A time for science: Past and present in the reconstruction of Hindu science 1860–1920. In D. Ali (Ed.), *Invoking the past: The uses of history in South Asia*. New Delhi: Oxford University Press.

Arnold, J. (Director). (1955). *Tarantula* [Motion Picture]. USA: Universal International Pictures.

———. (Director). (1957). *The incredible shrinking man* [Motion Picture]. USA: Universal International Pictures.

Athique, A. (July 2011). From cinema hall to multiplex: A public history. *South Asian Popular Culture, 9*(2), 147–160.

Baker, R. W. (Director). (1973). *And now the screaming starts* [Motion Picture]. UK: Amicus Productions.

Bakhtin, M. (1986). *Speech genre and other late essays* (V. W. McGee, Trans.). Austin: University of Texas Press.

Balan, S. S. (Director). (1971). *Sanjog* [Motion Picture]. India: Bharati International.

Baldick, C. (2008). *Oxford dictionary of literary terms* (3rd edition). New York: Oxford University Press Inc.

Barretto, G., & Mohla, A. (Directors). (2006). *Jaane hoga kya?* [Motion Picture]. India: P.K. Arts Creations.

Bedi, P. J. (Director). (2012). *Ghost* [Motion Picture]. India: Venus Movies.

Benegal, S. (2007). Secularism and popular Indian culture. In A. D. Needham & R. S. Rajan (Eds), *Crisis of secularism in India* (pp. 225–238). Durham: Duke University Press.

Benei, V. (2008). 'Globalization' and regional(Ist) cinema in Western India: Public culture, private media, and the representation of a hindu national(Ist) hero, 1930s–2000s. *South Asian Popular Culture, 6*(2), 83–108.

Berger, J. (2008). *Ways of seeing*. London: Penguin and British Broadcasting Corporation.

Bernds, E. L. (Director). (1959). *Return of the fly* [Motion Picture]. USA: Associated Producers (API).

Bhakri, M. (Director). (1985). *Cheekh* [Motion Picture]. India: MKB Films.

Bhaneja, B. (1976). India's science and technology plan, 1974–79. *Social Studies of Science, 6*(1), 99–104.

Bhaskar, I., & Allen, R. (2009). *Islamicate culture of Bombay cinema*. New Delhi: Tulika Books.

Bhatt, M. (Director). (1992). *Junoon* [Motion Picture]. India: Vishesh Films.

Bhatt, V. (Director). (1965). *Himalay ki godmein* [Motion Picture]. India: Shri Prakash Films.

———. (Director). (2002). *Raaz* [Motion Picture]. India: Bhatt Productions, Tips Films Pvt. Ltd, Vishesh Films, Vishresh Entertainment.

———. (Director). (2008). *1920* [Motion Picture]. India: ASA Production & Enterprises.

———. (Director). (2010). *Shaapit: The Cursed* [Motion Picture]. India: ASA Production & Enterprises.

Bhatt, V. (Director). (2011). *Haunted* [Motion Picture]. India: ASA Production & Enterprises, BVG Films, DAR Motion Pictures.

Bohra, D. (Director). (1990). *Kafan* [Motion Picture]. India: Roop Combine.

Brij (Director). (1966). *Yeh raat phir na aaygi* [Motion Picture]. India: Shri Krishna Films.

Brophy, P. (1986). Horrality: The textuality of the contemporary horror film. *Screen, 27*(1), 2–13.

Brown, T. (2011). Spectacle and value in classical Hollywood cinema. In L. Hubner (Ed.), *Valuing films: Shifting perceptions of worth* (pp. 49–66). London: Palgrave Macmillan.

Buckland, W. (2012). *Film theory: Rational reconstructions.* New York: Routledge.

Cameroon, J. (Director). (1986). *Alien* [Motion Picture]. USA: Twentieth Century Fox Film Corporation, Brandywine Productions, SLM Production Group.

Carpenter, J. (Director). (1978). *Halloween* [Motion Picture]. USA: Compass International Pictures, Falcon International Productions.

———. (Director). (1994). *In the mouth of madness* [Motion Picture]. USA: New Line Cinema.

———. (Director). (1998). *Vampires* [Motion Picture]. USA: Film Office, JVC Entertainment Networks, Largo Entertainment, Spooky Tooth Productions, Storm King Productions.

Carroll, N. (1990). *The philosophy of horror or padadoxes of the heart.* London: Routledge.

Castle, W. (Director). (1959). *The tingler* [Motion Picture]. USA: Columbia Pictures, William Castle Productions.

Caughie, J. (1981). Autuer-structuralism. In J. Caughie (Ed.), *Theories of authorship: A reader* (pp. 123–130). London: British Film Institute.

Chakravarty, S. (1993). *National identity in popular Indian cinema 1947–1987.* Austin: University of Texas Press.

Chatterjee, P. (1989). The nationalist resolution of the women's question. In S. Vaid & K. Sangari (Eds), *Recasting women: Essays in Indian colonial history* (pp. 233–253). New Delhi: Kali for Women.

Chopra, B. R. (Director). (1980). *Insaaf ka tarazu* [Motion Picture]. India. B.R. Films.

———. (Director). (1990). *Mahabharata* [Motion Picture]. India: B. R. Films.

Chowdhry, P. (2000). *Colonial India and the making of empire cinema: Image, ideology and identity.* Manchester: Manchester University Press.

Clayton, J. (Director). (1961). *The innocents* [Motion Picture]. USA: Achilles, Twentieth Century Fox Film Corporation.

Clover, C. J. (1992). *Men, women and chain saws: Gender in the modern horror film.* Princeton: Princeton University Press.

Coates, P. (1988). *The double and the other: Identity as ideology as post-romantic fiction.* New York: St. Martin's Press.

Cook, P., & Bernink, M. (1999). *The cinema book.* London: British Film Institute.

Corman, R. (Director). (1961). *Pit and the pendulum* [Motion Picture]. USA: Alta Vista Productions.

———. (Director). (1963). *Haunted palace* [Motion Picture]. USA: Alta Vista, American International Pictures (AIP).

———. (Director). (1964). *Tomb of Ligeia* [Motion Picture]. USA: Alta Vista Film Production.

Crane, J. L. (1994). *Terror and the everyday life: Singular moments in the history of the horror film.* London: Sage.

Craven, W. (Director). (1984). *A Nightmare on Elm Street* [Motion Picture]. UK: New Line Cinema, Media Home Entertainment, Smart Egg Pictures.

Creed, B. (1993). *The monstrous feminine: Film, feminism, psychoanalysis.* London: Routledge.

———. (2002). Horror and the monstrous feminine: An imaginary abjection. In M. Jancovich (Ed.), *Horror the film reader* (pp. 67–76). London: Routledge.

———. (2015). Horror and the monstrous feminine: An imaginary abjection. In B. K. Grant (Ed.), *The dread of difference: Gender and the horror film* (2nd ed., pp. 37–67). Austin: University of Texas Press.

Cronenberg, D. (Director). (1979). *The brood* [Motion Picture]. Canada: Canadian Film Development Corporation (CFDC), Elgin International Films Ltd, Mutual Productions Ltd, Victor Solnicki Productions.

Cunningham, S. S. (Director). (1980). *Friday the 13th* [Motion Picture]. USA: Production Companies, Paramount Pictures (presents), Warner Bros, Georgetown Productions Inc., Sean S. Cunningham Films.

Dasgupta, C. (1989). Seeing and believing, science and mythology: Notes on the 'mythological' genre. *Film Quarterly, 42*(4), 12–18.

———. (1991). *The painted face: Studies in India's popular cinema.* New Delhi: Roli Books.

Dave, H. (Director). (1974). *Balak Dhruv* [Motion Picture]. India: Hodati Films.

Davis, R. H. (2005). The cultural background of hindutva. In A. Ayres & P. Oldenburg (Eds), *India briefing: Takeoff at last?* M.E. Sharpe.

Dawley, J. S. (Director). (1910). *Frankenstein* [Motion Picture]. USA: Edison Manufacturing Company.

dePalma, B. (Director). (1976). *Carrie* [Motion Picture]. USA: Red Bank Films.

Dhanoa, G. (Director). (2003). *Hawa* [Motion Picture]. India: Jeet's Entertainment.

Donner, R. (Director). (1976). *The omen* [Motion Picture]. USA: Twentieth Century Fox Film Corporation (presents) (as Twentieth Century-Fox). Twentieth Century-Fox Productions (made by) (as Twentieth Century-Fox Productions Limited), Mace Neufeld Productions.

Douglas, G. (Director). (1954). *Them!* [Motion Picture]. USA: Warner Bros.

D'Souza, L. (Director). (1996). *Paapi gudia* [Motion Picture]. India: Aum Films.

Dwyer, R. (2006). *Filming the gods: Religion and Indian cinema*. London: Routledge.

———. (2012). Bombay gothie: On the 60th anniversary of Kamal Amrohi's Mahal'. In R. Dwyer & J. Pinto (Eds), *Beyond the boundaries of Bollywood: The many forms of Hindi cinema* (2nd Impression edition). New Delhi: Oxford University Press.

Elsaesser, T. (1989). *New German cinema: A history*. London: Macmillan Education.

Faludi, S. (1992). *Backlash: The undeclared war against women*. London: Chatto & Windus.

Farmer, V. L. (2000). Depicting the nation: Media politics in independent India. In F. R. Frankel, Z. Hasan, R. Bhargava & B. Arora (Eds), *Transfroming India: Social and political dynamics of democracy*. New Delhi: Oxford University Press.

Fisher, T. (Director). (1959). *The hound of the Baskervilles* [Motion Picture]. UK: Hammers Films.

Florey, R. (Director). (1946). *The beast with five fingers* [Motion Picture]. USA: Warner Bros.

Foucault, M. (1973). *The order of things*. New York: Vintage.

———. (1978). *The history of sexuality: An introduction*. (R. Hurley, Trans.). Harmondsworth: Penguin.

———. (1979). *The history of sexuality* (Vol. 1). (R. Hurley, Trans.) London: Allen Lane.

———. (1998). *History of sexuality: The will to knowledge* (Vol. 1). London: Penguin.

———. (2012). *Archaeology of knowledge* (A. M. Sheridan, Trans.). (First Indian reprint edition). London: Routledge.

Francis, C. (Director). (1961). *The beast of Yucca Flats* [Motion Picture]. USA: Anthony Carduza.

Freitag, S. B. (2001). Vision of the nation: Theorizing the nexus between creation, consumption, and participation in the public sphere. In R. Dwyer & C. Pinney (Eds), *Pleasure and the Nation: The History, Politics and Consumption of Public Culture in India* (pp. 35–75). New Delhi: Oxford University Press.

Freud, S. (1960 [1923]). *The ego and the id.* (J. Riviere, Trans.) London: W.W. Norton & Co.

———. (1974). *Standard edition of the complete psychological works of Sigmund Freud.* (J. Strachey, Ed.). London: Hogarth Press.

———. (2001). The uncanny. In V. B. Leitch, W. E. Cain, L. A. Finke, B. E. Johnson & J. Mcgowan (Eds), *The norton anthology: Theory and criticism* (pp. 929–952). London: W.W. Norton & Company.

Friedkin, W. (Director). (1973). *The exorcist* [Motion Picture]. USA: Warner Bros, Hoya Productions.

Furie, S. J. (Director). (1982). *The entity* [Motion Picture]. USA: American Cinema Productions.

Gabriel, K. (2002). Draupadi's moment in Sita's syntax: Violations of the past and the construction of the community in Kamal Haasan's Hey Ram! In T. Abraham (Ed.), *Women and the politics of violence* (pp. 76–124). New Delhi: Har-Anand Publications Pvt. Ltd.

Ganti, T. (2009). The limits of decency and the decency of limits. In R. Kaur & W. Mazzarella (Eds), *Censorship in South Asia: Cultural regulation from sedition to seduction* (pp. 87–122). Indianapolis: Indiana University Press.

Gaonkar, D. P. (2001). On alternative modernities. In D. P. Goankar (Ed.), *Alternative modernities* (pp. 1–23). Durham: Duke University Press.

Geraghty, L. (2009). In J. White & S. Haenni (Eds), *Fifty Key American Films.* London: Routledge.

Gillman, S. (2003). *Blood talk: American race melodrama and the culture of the occult.* Chicago: University of Chicago Press.

Gledhill, C. (1999). History of genre criticism. In P. Cook & M. Bernink (Eds), *The cinema book* (pp. 137–147). London: British Film Institute.

Gopal, S. (2011). *Conjugations: Marriage and from in new Bollywood cinema.* Chicago: University of Chicago Press.

Gordon, B. (Director). (1957). *The amazing colossal man* [Motion Picture]. USA: Malibu Productions.

Gould, W. (2004). *Hindu nationalism and the language of politics in late colonial India.* London: Cambridge University Press.

Guenon, R. (2004). *Studies in hinduism* (S. D. Fohrs, Ed., & H. D. Fohrs, Trans.). New York: Sophia Perennis Et Universalis.

Gunning, T. (2010). Shadow play and dripping teat: The night of the hunter (1955). In T. Brown & J. Walters (Eds), *Film moments* (pp. 5–7). London: Palgrave Macmillan on behalf of British Film Institute.

Gupta, D. (8 November 2010). Why hinduism is science-proof. *The Times of India.* Retrieved 3 March 2014 from http://timesofindia. indiatimes.com/home/opinion/edit-page/Why-Hinduism-Is-Science-proof/articleshow/6884126.cms?referral=PM

Hall, J. (2001). The benefits of hindsight: Revisions of HUAC and the film and television industries in the front and guilty by suspicion. *Film quarterly, 54*(2), 15–26.

Hall, S. (1980). Encoding/decoding. In S. Hall, D. Hobson, A. Lowe & P. Willis (Eds), *Culture, media, language* (pp. 107–116). London: Routledge in association with the Centre for Contemporary Cultural Studies, University of Birmingham.

———. (1982). The rediscovery of ideology: The return of the 'repressed' in media studies. In M. Gurevitch, T. Bennett, J. Curran & J. Wollacott (Eds), *Culture, society and the media* (pp. 22–49). London: Methuen.

———. (1997). The work of representation. In S. Hall (Ed.), *Representation: Cultural representation and signifying practices* (pp. 13–74). London: Sage Publications Inc.

Hansen, K. (2002). Parsi theater and the city. *Sarai Reader 2000: The Cities of Everyday Life*, 40–49.

Hardwicke, C. (Director). (2008). *Twilight* [Motion Picture]. USA: Summit Entertainment (presents), Temple Hill Entertainment (as Temple Hill), Maverick Films (in association with) (as Maverick), Imprint Entertainment (in association with) (as Imprint), Goldcrest Pictures (in association with), Twilight Productions.

Harpham, J. G. (2006). *On the grotesque: Strategies of contradiction in art and literature*. Colarado: Davies Group Publishers.

Haskins, B. (Director). (1953). *War of the worlds* [Motion Picture]. USA: Paramount Pictures.

Haynes, J. (1999). *Religion, globalization and the political culture in the third world*. London: Palgrave.

Hayward, S. (1996). *Key concepts in cinema studies*. London: Routledge.

———. (2006). *Cinema studies: The key concepts* (3rd edition). London: Routledge.

Heffernan, J. A. (1997). Looking at the monster: Frankenstein and film. *Critical Inquiry, 24*(1), 133–158.

Hitchcock, A. (Director). (1940). *Rebecca* [Motion Picture]. USA: Selznick International Pictures.

———. (Director). (1960). *Psycho* [Motion Picture]. USA: Shamley Productions.

Hogle, J. E. (2002). Introduction. In J. E. Hogle (Ed.), *The Cambridge companion to gothic fiction* (pp. 1–20). London: Cambridge University Press.

Holland, T. (Director). (1985). *Fright night* [Motion Picture]. USA: Columbia Pictures (presents), Vistar Films, Columbia Pictures Industries (from) (as Columbia-Delphi IV Productions), Delphi IV Productions (from) (as Columbia-Delphi IV Productions).

Holquist, M. (2010). *Dialogism: Bakhtin and his world.* London: Routledge.

Hughes, S. (2006). House full: Silent film genre, exhibition and audiences in South India. *Indian Economic & Social History Review, 43*(1), 31–62.

Hyams, P. (Director). (1999). *End of days* [Motion Picture]. USA: Beacon Pictures.

Inamdar, I., & Misra, A. K. (Directors). (1988). *Pyaasi aatma* [Motion Picture]. India: Sakhee Lal Movies.

Indian Cinematograph Committee. (1928). *Report of the Indian cinematograph committee 1927–28.* Calcutta: Government of India, Central Publications Branch.

Ingebretsen, E. J. (1998). Staking the monster: A politics of remonstrance. *Religion and American Culture: A Journal of Interpretation, 8*(1), 91–116.

Ishaara, B. R. (Director). (1988). *Woh phir aayegi* [Motion Picture]. India: Jay Vijay Enterprises.

Iyer, K. (Director). (2013). *Ek thi daayan* [Motion Picture]. India: ALT Entertainment, Balaji Motion Pictures, Vishal Bhardwaj Pictures.

Jaffrelot, C. (1996). *The Hindu nationalist movement and Indian politics 1925 to the 1990s.* London: C. Hurst & Co.

Jain, B. (Director). (2014). *Six minus five equals two* [Motion Picture]. India: Mars Inc.

Jancovich, M. (2002). General Introduction. In *The horror film reader.* London: Routledge.

———. (2009). Thrills and chills: Horror, the woman's film, and the origins of film noir. *New Review of Film and Television Studies, 7*(2), 157–171.

Jean-Baptiste, A., & Canepa, F. (Directors). (2003). *Dead end* [Motion Picture]. France: Pentagon Pictures.

Jermyn, D. (1996). Rereading the bitches from hell: A feminist appropriation of the female psychopath. *Screen, 37*(3), 251–67.

Jordan, R. (2007). Case study: Film sound, acoustic ecology and performance in electroacoustic music. In J. Sexton (Ed.), *Music sound and the multimedia: From the live to the virtual* (pp. 121–144). Edinburgh: Edinburgh University Press.

Julian, R. (Director). (1925). *The phamtom of the opera* [Motion Picture]. USA: Universal Pictures.

Kapur, S. (Director). (1987). *Mr. India* [Motion Picture]. India: Narsimha Enterprises.

Kashyap, A. (Director). (1992). *Maa* [Motion Picture]. India: Shantketan Film Combines.

Katovich, M. A., & Kinkade, P. T. (1993). The stories told in science fiction and social science: Reading "the thing" and other remakes. *The Sociological Quarterly, 34*(4), 619–637.

Kaushik, K. (Director). (2010). *Hum tum aur ghost* (me, you and the ghost) [Motion Picture]. India: Movie Vision Entertainment, Shooting Stars Productions, Studio 18.

Kaushik, S. (Director). (2014). *Gang of ghosts* [Motion Picture]. India: Venus Reords & Tapes.

Kaviraj, S. (1997). *Politics in India.* New Delhi: Oxford University Press.

Kavka, M. (2002). The gothic on screen. In J. E. Hogle (Ed.), *The cambridge guide to gothic fiction* (pp. 209–228). Cambridge: Cambridge University Press.

Kelleter, F., & Mayer, R. (2007). The melodramatic mode revisted. An introduction. In F. Kelleter, B. Krah & R. Mayer (Eds), *Melodrama! The mode of excess from early America to Hollywood* (Vol. 145, pp. 7–18). Heidelberg: Universitatsverlag.

Kellner, D. (1996). Poltergeists, gender and class in the age of Reagan and Bush. In D. E. James & R. Berg (Eds), *The hidden foundation* (pp. 217–239). Minneapolis: University of Minneapolis Press.

Kenton, E. C. (Director). (1932). *Island of lost souls* [Motion Picture]. USA: Paramount Pictures.

———. (Director). (1945). *House of dracula* [Motion Picture]. USA: Universal Pictures.

Khan, S. (Director). (1999). *Hello brother* [Motion Picture]. India: G. S. Entertainment.

Khosla, R. (Director). (1964). *Woh kaun thi?* [Motion Picture]. India: Prithvi Pictures.

King, S. (n.d.). *Why we crave horror movies.* Retrieved 29 March 2012, from http://drmarkwomack.com/pdfs/horrormovies.pdf

Kohli, R. (Director). (1976). *Nagin* [Motion Picture]. India: Shankar Films.

———. (Director). (1979). *Jaani dushman* [Motion Picture]. India: Shankar Films.

———. (Director). (1988). *Bees saal baad* [Motion Picture]. India: Nishi Productions.

Kripalani, P. (Director). (2011). *Ragini MMS* [Motion Picture]. India: ALT Entertainment, Balaji Telefilms, iRock Films (as iRock Bollywood Entertainment).

Kristeva, J. (1982). *Powers of horror: An essay of abjection.* (L. S. Rudiez, Trans.). New York: Columbia University Press.

Kuhn, A., & Westwell, G. (2012). *Dictionary of film studies.* London: Oxford University Press.

Kumar, M. (Director). (1967). *Upkaar* [Motion Picture]. India: Modern Studios, V.I.P. Films (as Vishal Pictures).

———. (Director). (1970). *Purab aur paschim* [Motion Picture]. India. V.I.P Films.

Kumar, P. (Director). (1993). *Zakhmi rooh* [Motion Picture]. India: Hemanshu Films Combine.

Kumar, R. (Director). (1992). *Suryavanshi* [Motion Picture]. India: Sainath Films International.

Kumar, V. K. (Director). (2009). *13B* [Motion Picture]. India: Reliance Big Pictures.

Landers, L. (Director). (1944). *The return of the vampire* [Motion Picture]. USA: Columbia Pcitures Corporation.

Laplanche, J., & Pontalis, J. B. (1973). *The language of psychoanalysis*. Exeter: The Hogarth Press Ltd.

Lawrence, F. (Director). (2005). *Constantine* [Motion Picture]. USA/ Germany: Warner Bros, Village Roadshow Pictures, DC Comics (Vertigo), Lonely Film Productions GmbH & Co. KG, Donners' Company, Branded Entertainment/Batfilm Productions, Weed Road Pictures, 3 Arts Entertainment, Di Bonaventura Pictures.

Lester, I. (6 October 2007). Abortion: Still a feminist issue. *The F word: Contemporary Feminism UK*. Retrieved 25 September 2012, from http://www.thefword.org.uk/features/2007/10/abortion_still

Levi-Strauss, C. (1963). *Structural anthropology*. (C. Jacobson & B. G. Schoepf, Trans.). New York: Basic Books.

———. (1970). *The raw and the cooked: Introduction to a science of mythology*. (J. Weightman & D. Weightman, Trans.). London: Jonathan Cape.

Lipner, J. (1989). The classical Hindu view on abortion and the moral status of theu. In *Hindu ethics: Purity, abortion and euthanasia* (pp. 41–70). Albany: New York State University Press.

Lipsitz, G. (1998). Genre anxiety and racial representation in 1970s cinema. In N. Browne (Ed.), *Refiguring American film genres: Theory and history* (pp. 216–220). Los Angeles: University of California Press.

Louis, W. (Director). (2009). *Mallika* [Motion Picture]. India: PPC Horrotainment in association with Glorious entertainment.

———. (Director). (2010). *Kaalo* [Motion Picture]. India: Beyond Dreams Entertainment, Jai Jagannath Pictures (in association with).

Lourie, E. (Director). (1953). *The beast from 20,000 fathoms* [Motion Picture]. USA: Jack Dietz Productions (as Mutual Pictures of California).

Lowenstein, A. (2010). Living dead: Fearful attractions of film. *Representations, 110*(1), 105–128.

Madhukar, H. (Director). (2014). *Mumbai 125 KM* [Motion Picture]. India: A Light and Shadow Films.

Majumder, R. (2012). Ramsay International. *Motherland*. Retrieved 11 May 2014, from http://www.motherlandmagazine.com/ghost-issue/ramsay-international

Malhotra, B. K. (Director). (1998). *Ek raat shaitaan ke saath* [Motion Picture]. India: Heeros Film combine.

Malhotra, S., & Alagh, T. (2004). Dreaming the nation: Domestic dramas in Hindi films. *South Asian Popular culture, 2*(1), 19–37.

Mankekar, P. (1999). *Screening culture, viewing politics: An ethnography of television, womanhood and nation in postcolonial India.* Durnham: Duke University Press.

———. (2004). Dangerous desires: Television and erotics in late twentieth-century India. *The Journal of Asian Studies, 63*(2), 403–415.

Marcuse, H. (1955). *Eros and civilization.* London: Sphere Books.

Marnau, F. W. (Director). (1922). *Nosferatu* [Motion Picture]. Germany: Jofa-Atelier Berlin-Johannisthal, Prana-Film GmbH.

Mazzarella, W. (2009). Making Sense of the cinema in late colonial India. In R. Kaur & W. Mazzarella (Eds), *Censorship in South Asia: Cultural regulation from sedition to seduction* (pp. 63–86). Indianapolis: Indian University Press.

Mehra, R. (Director). (1992). *Chamatkar* [Motion Picture]. India: Eagle Films (presents), United Producers.

Menon, N. (2004). *Recovering subversion: Feminist politics beyond the law.* New Delhi: Permanent Black.

Mishra, P. (21 August 2005). How India reconciles hindu values and biotech. *The New York Times.* Retrieved 15 February 2014, fromhttp://www.nytimes.com/2005/08/21/weekinreview/21mishra.html?pagewanted=all&_r=0

Mishra, V. (2002). *Bollywood cinema: Temples of desire.* London: Routledge.

Mistry, B. (Director). (1970). *Bhagwan Parshuram* (Lord Parshuram) [Motion Picture]. India: Mewar Films.

Morakhia, S. (Director). (2005). *Naina* [Motion Picture]. India: iDream Productions.

Morgan, K. W. (1987). *The religion of the hindus.* New Delhi: Motilal Banarsidass.

Mubarki, M. A. (2013). Mapping the hindi horror genre: ghosts in the service of ideology. *History and Sociology of South Asia, 7*(1), 39–60.

Mukhopadhyay, U. (2008). Communalism, secularism and the Indian historical films (1940–1946). *Economic and Political Weekly, 43*(15), 63–71.

Mulvey, L. (1989). Visual pleasure and narrative cinema. In L. Mulvey, *Visual and other pleasures: Collected essays* (pp. 14–26). London: Macmillan.

Nag, B. (Director). (1962). *Bees saal baad* [Motion Picture]. India: Geetanjali Pictures.

———. (Director). (1964). *Kohraa* [Motion Picture]. India: Geetanjali Pictures.

Nagaich, R. (Director). (1967). *Farz* [Motion Picture]. India: Vijayalakshmi Pictures.

Nagaich, R. (Director). (1977). *Jadu tona* [Motion Picture]. India: Guru Enterprising Movies.

Nagl, M. (1983). The science fiction film in historical perspective. (RMP, Ed.) *Science Fiction Studies, 10*(3), 262–277.

Nair, K. (2009). Run for your lives: Remembering the Ramsay brothers. In R. Franklin & R. Richardson (Eds), *The many forms of fear, horror and terror.* Inter-Disciplinary Press.

Nanda, M. (1998). Reclaiming modern science for third world progressive social movements. *Economic And Political Weekly, 33*(16), 915–922.

———. (1999). Debate over science: Moving past politics of nostalgia. *Economic and Political Weekly, 34*(18), 1065–1068.

Nandy, A. (1998). Indian cinema as a slum's eye view of politics. In A. Nandy (Ed.), *The secret politics of our desires: Innocence, culpability and Indian popular cinema* (pp. 1–18). Palgrave Macmillan.

Narang, S. (Director). (2004). *Vaastu shastra* [Motion Picture]. India: K Sera Sera, Varma Productions.

Naremore, J. (1995). American film noir: The history of an idea. *Film Quarterly, 49*(2), pp. 12–28.

Neale, S. (1980). *Genre.* London: British Film Institute.

Neelam, J. (Director). (2002). *Kunwari chudail* [Motion Picture]. India: Deep Jyoti Films.

Nehru, J. (2004). *The discovery of India.* New Delhi: Penguin Books.

Neumann, K. (Director). (1958). *The fly* [Motion Picture]. India: Twentieth Century Fox Film Corporation.

Nidimoru, R., & Krishna, D. K. (Directors). (2013). *Go Goa gone* [Motion Picture]. India: D2R Films, Eros International, Illuminati Films.

Nikhilananda S. (Trans.). *Svetasvatara Upanishad* (n.d.). Retrieved 29 March 2013, from http://www.bharatadesam.com/spiritual/upanishads/svetasvatara_upanishad.php

Noorani, A. G. (2006). *Constitutional questions and citizen's rights: An omnibus comprising constitutional questions in India.* New Delhi: Oxford University Press.

Norrington, S. (Director). (1998). *Blade* [Motion Picture]. USA: New Line Cinemas

Nowell-Smith, G. (1970). Cinema and structuralism. *20th Century Studies, 3*(May), 131–139.

Palekar, A. (Director). (2005). *Paheli* [Motion Picture]. India: Red Chillies Entertainment.

Patel, A., & Dave, Y. (Directors). (2012). *?: Question mark* [Motion Picture]. India: Triple Take Motion Pictures.

Patel, B. (Director). (2012). *1920: The evil returns* [Motion Picture]. India: ASA Production & Enterprises, BVG Films.

———. (Director). (2014). *Ragini MMS 2* [Motion Picture]. India: ALT Entertainment, Balaji Motion Pictures.

Patel, B. (Director). (2015). *Alone* [Motion Picture]. India: Panorama Studios.

Phalke, D. (Director). 1913. *Raja Harishchandra* [Motion Picture]. India: Phalke films.

Phat, D. P., & Chun, O. P. (Directors). (2002). *The eye* [Motion Picture]. Hong Kong/Singapore: Applause Pictures (present), Mediacorp Raintree Pictures (as Raintree Pictures).

Pinney, C. (2009). Iatronic religion and politics. In R. Kaur & W. Mazzarella (Eds), *Censorship in South Asia: Cultural regulation from sedition to seduction* (pp. 29–62). Bloomington: Indian University Press.

Pisanthanakun, B., & Wongpoom, P. (Directors). (2004). *Shutter* (espiritos-A morte está ao seu lado) [Motion Picture]. Thailand: GMM Pictures Co., Phenomena (as Phenomena Motion Pictures).

Pisanthanakun, B., & Wongpoom, P. (Directors). (2007). *Alone*. [Motion Picture]. Thailand: Dedicate Ltd. GMM, Phenomena.

Polanski, R. (Director). (1965). *Repulsion* [Motion Picture]. UK: A Compton Productions.

Powell, M. (Director). (1960). *Peeping tom* [Motion Picture]. UK: A Compton Productions.

Prasad, M. M. (2000). *Ideology of the Hindi film: A historical construction.* New Delhi: Oxford University Press.

————. (2004). The natives are looking: Cinema and censorship in colonial India. In L. J. Moran, E. Sandon, E. Loizidou & I. Christie (Eds), *Law's moving image* (pp. 161–172). London: The Glasshouse Press.

Priyadarshan (Director). (2007). *Bhool bhulaiyaa* [Motion Picture]. India: Super Cassettes Industries Limited.

Rafi (Director). (1998). *Pyaasi chudail* [Motion Picture]. India: Salgia & Co.

Raimi, S. (Director). (1987). *Evil dead II: Dead by dawn* [Motion Picture]. USA: De Laurentiis Entertainment Group (DEG), Renaissance Pictures.

Raina, A. (Director). (2013). *Horror story* [Motion Picture]. India: ASA Production & Enterprises Pvt. Ltd.

Rajadhyaksha, A. (1999). Hindi cinema. In P. Cook & M. Bernink (Eds), *The cinema book* (pp. 130–134). London: British Film Institute.

Rajagopal, A. (2001). *Politics after television: Hindu nationalism and the reshaping of the public in India.* Cambridge: Cambridge University Press.

Rajasthani, M. M. (2006). *Effectuation of Shani adoration.* New Delhi: Saturn Publications Pvt. Ltd.

Raje, A., & Desai, V. (Directors). (1980). *Gehrayee* [Motion Picture]. India: Avikam.

Raman, P. (Director). (2011). *404: Error not found* [Motion Picture]. India: APCA News & Entertainment, Imagik Media.

Ramaswamy, S. (2001). Maps and mother goddesses in modern India. *Imago Mundo, 53*(1), 97–114.

Ramsay, D. (Director). (2006). *Aatma* [Motion Picture]. India: Parallel Films, Tulsi Ramsay Productions.

Ramsay, K. (Director). (1987). *Dak bangla* [Motion Picture]. India: Ramsay Productions.

———. (Director). (1990). *Shaitani ilaaka* [Motion Picture]. India: Ramsay Productions.

Ramsay, S. (Director). (2003). *Dhund* [Motion Picture]. India: Sukrit Pictures.

Ramsay, S., & Ramsay, T. (Directors). (1978). *Darwaza* [Motion Picture]. India: Ramsay Productions.

———. (Directors). (1980). *Saboot* [Motion Picture]. India: Abbasi Bros (presented by), The Bharat Pictures.

———. (Directors). (1981). *Hotel* [Motion Picture]. India: Vision Universal.

———. (Directors). (1989). *Purani haveli* [Motion Picture]. India: Ramsay International.

———. (Directors). (1993). *Mahakaal* [Motion Picture]. India: Cine Films, Prerna Films, Ramsay Productions (as Ramsay Cine).

Ramsay, T. (Director). (1972). *Do gaz zameen ke neeche* [Motion Picture]. India: Ramsay Films.

Ramsay, T., & Ramsay, S. (Directors). (1980). *Guest house* [Motion Picture]. India: Ramsay Productions.

———. (Directors). (1981). *Dahshat* [Motion Picture]. India: Ramsay Productions.

———. (Directors). (1988). *Veerana* [Motion Picture]. India: Sai Om Productions.

———. (Directors). (1990). *Bandh darwaza* [Motion Picture]. India: Ramsay Productions.

Ransinghe, R. (Director). (2010). *Rokk* [Motion Picture]. India: Ikkon Films.

Rao, T. R. (Director). (1982). *Jeevandhara* [Motion Picture]. India: Prasad Art Pictures.

———. (Director). (1983). *Mujhe insaaf chahiye* [Motion Picture]. India: D.V.S. Productions.

Razdan, K. (Director). (2006). *Eight: The power of Shani* [Motion Picture]. India: United Dream Entertainments.

Real, M. (1989). *Super media*. London: Sage Publications.

Robinson, W. C. (May 2003). *Risks and rights: The causes, consequences and challenges of development induced displacement*. Washington: The Brookings Institution-SAIS Project on Internal Displacement.

Robson, M. (Director). (1945). *The isle of the dead* [Motion Picture]. USA: RKO Radio Pictures.

Romero, G. A. (Director). (1969). *Night of the living dead* [Motion Picture]. USA: Image Ten (as an Image Ten Production), Laurel Group, Market Square Productions, Off Color Films.

Roshan, R. (Director). (2003). *Koi mil gaya* [Motion Picture]. India: Film Kraft, Films & Casting Temple Pvt. Ltd. Sydney: Australian Production Company.

———. (Director). (2006). *Krrish* [Motion Picture]. India: Film Kraft.

———. (Director). (2013). *Krrish 3* [Motion Picture]. India: Film Kraft.

Roy, B. (Director). (1958). *Madhumati* [Motion Picture]. India: Bimal Roy Productions.

Rudolph, L., & Rudolph, S. (1987). *In pursuit of Lakshmi: The political economy of the Indian state.* New Delhi: Orient Longman.

Ryall, T. (1978). *Teacher's study guide no. 2: The gangester's film.* London: BFI Education.

Sagar, R. (Director). (1968). *Aakhen* [Motion Picture]. India: Sagar Art International.

———. (Director). (1972). *Lalkar* [Motion Picture]. India: Sagar Art International.

———. (Director). (1987). *Ramayana* [Motion Picture]. India: Sagar Enterprises.

Sahu, K. (Director). (1965). *Poonam ki raat* [Motion Picture]. India: Kishore Sahu Productions.

Salva, V. (Director). (2001). *Jeepers creepers* [Motion Picture]. India: United Artists (presents) (as United Artists Films), American Zoetrope, Cinerenta-Cinebeta, Cinerenta Medienbeteiligungs KG (in association with), VCL Communications.

Sarkar, S. (2002). *Beyond nationalist frames: Relocating postmodern history.* New Delhi: Permanent Black.

Savran, D. (1998). *Taking it like a man: White masculinity, maschochism, and contemporary American culture.* New Jersey: Princeton University Press.

Sayed, N. (Director). (1992). *Yeh raat phir na aayegi* [Motion Picture]. India: Zakir Hussain Films.

Sayed, S. U. (Director). (1989). *Saat saal baad* [Motion Picture]. India: Naseem Enterprises.

Sconce, J. (1993). Spectacle of death: Identification, reflexivity and contemporary horror. In J. Collins, H. Radner & A. P. Collins (Eds), *Film theory goes to the movies* (pp. 103–119). London: Routledge.

Sen, I. (2002). *Woman and empire: Representations in the writings of colonial India (1858–1900).* New Delhi: Orient Longman.

Sen, M. (2011). *Terrifying tots and hapless homes: Undoing modernity in recent Bollywood cinema.* Literature Interpretation Theory, 22(3), 197–217.

Sethumadhavan, K. S. (Director). (1975). *Julie* [Motion Picture]. India: Vijaya Productions Pvt. Ltd.

Sharma, D. (1976). Growth and failures of India's science policy. *Economic and Political Weekly, 11*(51), 1961–1971.

Sharma, M. (2011). *Green and saffron: Hindu nationalism and Indian environmental politics.* New Delhi: Permanent Black.

Sharma, S. R. (Director). (1965). *Shaheed* [Motion Picture]. India: K.P.K. Movies.

Sharma, V. (Director). (1975). *Jai Santoshi maa* [Motion Picture]. India: Bhagyalakshmi Chitra Mandir.

———. (Director). (2008). *Bhootnath* [Motion Picture]. India: B.R. Films.

Sharyananda, S. (Trans.). (1921). *Taittiriya Upanishad.* Madras: The Ramakrishna Math.

Shelly, J. (Director). (1986). *Aadamkhor* [Motion Picture]. India: Hargobindha Films.

Shimizu, T. (Director). (2002). *Juon* [Motion Picture]. Japan: Pioneer LDC, Nikkatsu, Oz Company, Xanadeux.

———. (Director). (2004). *The grudge* [Motion Picture]. USA/Japan: Columbia Pictures (presents), Ghost House Pictures (production).

Shrivastava, S. (2007). *Passionate modernity: Sexuality, class and consumption in India.* Routledge.

Siegel, D. (Director). (1956). *Invasion of the boby snatchers* [Motion Picture]. USA: Walter Wanger Productions.

Singh, B. (2008). Aadamkhor haseena (man eating beauty) and the anthropology of the moment. *Contribution to Indian Sociology, 42*(2), 249–279.

Singhal, A., & Rogers, E. M. (2001). *India's communication revolution: From bullock carts to cyber marts.* New Delhi: SAGE Publications.

Sinha, A. (Director). (2011). *Ra.One* [Motion Picture]. India: Red Chillies Entertainment.

Sinha, B. (2011). Empire films and the dissemination of americanism in colonial India. *South Asian History and Culture, 2*(4), 540–556.

Sivan, S. (Director). (2010). *Click* [Motion Picture]. India: M/s Rupali Aum Entertainment, PVR Pictures Ltd., Pritish Nandy Communications (PNC), RNA Play Entertainment, Sangeeth Sivan Productions.

Smelik, A. (1999). Feminist film theory. In P. Cook & M. Bernink (Eds), *The cinema book* (2nd edition, pp. 353–362). London: British Film Institute.

Sobchack, V. (1996). The fantastic. In G. N. Smith (Ed.), *The oxford history of world cinema* (pp. 312–321). London: Oxford University Press.

———. (2001). *Screening space: The American science fiction film* (4th reprint edition). New Jersey: Rutgers University Press.

Sommers, S. (Director). (1999). *The mummy* [Motion Picture]. USA: Universal Pictures, Alphaville Films.

———. (Director). (2004). *Van Helsing* [Motion Picture]. USA: Universal Pictures.

Soni, S. (Director). (1964). *Mr. X in Bombay* [Motion Picture]. India: Thakkar Films.

———. (Director). (1965). *Shreeman Funtoosh* [Motion Picture]. India: S. B. Productions.

Srinivas, M. N. (1984). *Social change in modern India*. New Delhi: Orient Longman.

Srivastava, N. (2008). *Secularism in the postcolonial Indian novel* (1st Indian reprint edition). New Delhi: Routledge.

Starks, L. S. (2002). "Remember me": Psychoanalysis, cinema and the crisis of modernity. *Shakespeare Quarterly, 53*(2), 181–200.

Sundaram, T. P. (Director). (1967). *Chand par chadayee* [Motion Picture]. India: Cauvery Productions.

Suri, M. (Director). (2009). *Raaz: The mystery continues* [Motion Picture]. India: Sony BMG, Vishesh Films.

Syed, S. U. (Director). (1979). *Bhayanak* [Motion Picture]. India: AVM Arts International.

Talwar, V. (Director). (1989). *Wohi bhayanak raat* [Motion Picture]. India: Talwar Productions.

Tilak, R. (Director). (1981). *Chehre pe chehra* [Motion Picture]. India: Tilak Movies' Pvt. Ltd.

Time. (1952). End of the Zammdars. *Time.* 14 July.

Tiwari, N. (Director). (2014). *Bhoothnath returns* [Motion Picture]. India: B. R. Films, T-Series.

Toro, G. D. (Director). (2004). *Hellboy* [Motion Picture]. USA: Revolution Studios (presents), Lawrence Gordon Productions, Starlite Films, Dark Horse Entertainment (in association with).

Trifonova, T. (2010). Multiple personality and the discourse of the multpiple in Hollywood cinema. *European Journal of American Culture, 29*(2), 145–171.

Tudor, A. (1989). *Monsters and mad scientists: A cultural history of the horror film*. Oxford and New York: B. Blackwell.

———. (1997). Why horror? The peculiar pleasures of a popular genre. *Cultural Studies, 11*(3), 443–463.

Twitchell, J. (1985). *Dreadful pleasures: An anatomy of modern horror*. Oxford: Oxford University Press.

Upadhyay, V. S., & Pandey, G. (1993). *History of Anthropological Thought*. New Delhi: Concept Publishing House.

Upadhyaya, P. C. (1992). The politics of Indian secularism. *Modern Asian Studies, 26*(4), 815–53.

Varadpande, M. L. (1992). *History of Indian theatre: Loka ranga panorama of Indian folk theatre*. New Delhi: Abhinav Publications.

Varma, R. G. (Director). (1992). *Raat* [Motion Picture]. India: Varma Films.

———. (Director). (2003). *Bhoot* [Motion Picture]. India: Dream Merchants Enterprise (as Dream Merchants), Varma Corporation.

Varma, R. G. (Director). (2004). *Vaastu shastra* [Motion Picture]. India: K Sera Sera, Varma Corporation.

———. (Director). (2007). *Darling* [Motion Picture]. India: T-Series Films.

———. (Director). (2008). *Phoonk* [Motion Picture]. India: Ace Movie Company, One More Thought Entertainment (as One More Thought Entertainment Pvt. Ltd.)

Varma, S. (Director). (2004). *Krishna cottage* [Motion Picture]. India: Balaji motion.

Vasudevan, R. (2000). The politics of cultural address in a 'transitional' cinema : A case study of Indian popular cinema. In C. Gledhill & L. Williams (Eds), *Reinventing film theory* (pp. 130–164). London: Arnold.

———. (2003). Cinema in urban space. Retrieved 17 May 2014, from http://www.india-seminar.com/2003/525/525%20ravi%20vasudevan.htm

Vijay, B. (Director). (1981). *Mangalsutra* [Motion Picture]. India: Gaurav Films International.

Virani, R. (Director). (2010). *Help* [Motion Picture]. India: Rupali Aum Entertainment Pvt. Ltd.

Virdi, J. (2003). *The cinematic imagination: Indian popular films as social history*. New Delhi: Permanent Black.

Vishwanath, G. (2002). Saffronizing the silver screen: The right-winged nineties film. In J. Jain & S. Rai (Eds), *Film and feminism: Essays in Indian cinema*. Jaipur: Rawat Publications.

Wacquant, L. J. (2008). Pierre bourdieu. In R. Stones (Ed.), *Key sociological thinkers* (2nd edition, pp. 261–277). London: Palgrave Macmillan.

Warshow, R. (2002). *The immediate experience: Movies, comics, theatre and other aspects of popular culture*. Harvard University Press.

Whale, J. (Director). (1931). *Frankenstein* [Motion Picture]. USA: Universal Pictures.

———. (Director). (1935). *Bride of Frankenstein* [Motion Picture]. USA: Universal Pictures.

Wiederhorn, K. (Director). (1981). *Eye of a stranger* [Motion Picture]. USA: Georgetown Productions Inc.

Wiene, R. (Director). (1920). *The cabinet of Dr. Caligari* [Motion Picture]. Germany: Decla-Bioscop AG (as Decla Film-Gesellschaft - Berlin).

Williams, A. (2002). Introduction. In A. Williams (Ed.), *Film and Nnationalism* (pp. 1–22). New Jersey: Rutgers University Press.

Williams, L. (1981). Film madness: The uncanny return of the repressed in polanski's 'the tenant'. *Cinema Journal, 20*(2), 63–73.

———. (1991). Film bodies: Gender, genre, and excess. *Film Quarterly, 44*(4), 2–13.

———. (2002). When the woman looks. In M. Jankovich (Ed.), *Horror: The film reader* (pp. 61–66). New York: Routledge.

Wise, R. (Director). (1951). *The day the earth stood still* [Motion Picture]. USA: Twentieth Century Fox Film corporation.

———. (Director). (1963). *The haunting* [Motion Picture]. UK/USA: Argyle Enterprises.

Wise, R., & Fritsch, G. V. (Directors). (1944). *Curse of the cat people* [Motion Picture]. USA: RKO Radio Pictures.

Wiseman, L. (Director). (2003). *Underworld* [Motion Picture]. USA: Lakeshore Entertainment, Laurinfilm, Subterranean Productions LLC, Subterranean Productions UK Ltd, Underworld Productions GmbH.

Wood, R. (2003). *Hollywood from Vietnam to Reagan and beyond*. New York: Columbia University Press.

Wright, M. J. (2007). *Religion and film: An introduction*. London: I. B. Taurus & Co. Ltd.

Zemeckis, R. (Director). (2000). *What lies beneath* [Motion Picture]. USA: DreamWorks SKG (presents) (as DreamWorks Pictures), Twentieth Century Fox Film Corporation (presents) (as Twentieth Century Fox), ImageMovers.

Zimmer, H. (1992). *Myths and symbols in Indian art and civilization*. (J. Campbell, Ed.). New Jersey: Princeton University Press.

Index

About the Author

Meraj Ahmed Mubarki earned his Master's Degree and Doctorate in Journalism and Mass Communication from the University of Calcutta. He worked as a freelancer before moving into the academics. He has taught at various higher education institutions including Shri Shikshayatan College, Kolkata, and was the founding head of the Department of Journalism & Mass Communication. He is currently Assistant Professor in the Department of Mass Communication & Journalism at Maulana Azad National Urdu University, Hyderabad, where he teaches courses on film studies, advertising and market research, English journalistic skills and editing. He has contributed articles to renowned peer-reviewed international journals, such as *Contemporary South Asia, Indian Journal of Gender Studies, Media Asia, Visual Anthropology* and *History and Sociology of South Asia.* His research areas include gender, representation, ideology, cinema and genre studies.